OUT OF HEARING

WILEY SERIES
in
CHILD PROTECTION AND POLICY

Series Editor: Christopher Cloke, NSPCC,
42 Curtain Road,
London EC2A 3NX

The NSPCC/Wiley series explores current issues relating to the prevention of child abuse and the protection of children. The series aims to publish titles that focus on professional practice and policy, and the practical application of research. The books are leading edge and innovative and reflect a multi-disciplinary and inter-agency approach to the prevention of child abuse and the protection of children.

This series is essential reading for all professionals and researchers concerned with the prevention of child abuse and the protection of children. The accessible style will appeal to parents and carers. All books have a policy or practice orientation with referenced information from theory and research.

Published Titles

Bannister	From Hearing to Healing: Working with the Aftermath of Child Sexual Abuse, Second Edition	0-471-98298-9
Butler & Williamson	Children Speak: Child Trauma and Social Work	0-471-97219-3
Cloke & Davies	Participation and Empowerment in Child Protection	0-471-97218-5
Cloke & Nash	Key Issues in Child Protection for Health Visitors and Nurses	0-471-97217-7
Platt & Shemmings (in association with NISW & PAIN)	Making Enquiries into Alleged Child Abuse and Neglect: Partnership with Families	0-471-97222-3
Wattam	Making a Case in Child Protection	0-471-97225-8
Wattam, Hughes & Blagg	Child Sexual Abuse: Listening, Hearing and Validating the Experiences of Children	0-471-97281-9

Forthcoming Titles

Cloke	Primary Prevention of Child Abuse	0-471-97775-6
Parton & Wattam	Child Sexual Abuse: Responding to the Experiences of Children	0-471-98334-9

Potential authors are invited to submit ideas and proposals for publication in the series to Christopher Cloke, Series Editor.

OUT OF HEARING

Representing Children in Care
Proceedings

Judith Masson and
Maureen Winn Oakley

JOHN WILEY & SONS

Chichester · New York · Weinheim · Brisbane · Singapore · Toronto

Copyright © 1999 by John Wiley & Sons Ltd,
Baffins Lane, Chichester,
West Sussex PO19 1UD, England

National   01243 779777
International   (+44) 1243 779777
e-mail (for orders and customer service enquiries): cs-book@wiley.co.uk
Visit our Home Page on http://www.wiley.co.uk
or http://www.wiley.com

Other Wiley Editorial Offices

John Wiley & Sons, Inc., 605 Third Avenue,
New York, NY 10158-0012, USA

WILEY-VCH Verlag GmbH, Pappelallee 3,
D-69469 Weinheim, Germany

Jacaranda Wiley Ltd, 33 Park Road, Milton,
Queensland 4064, Australia

John Wiley & Sons (Asia) Pte Ltd, 2 Clementi Loop #02-01,
Jin Xing Distripark, Singapore 129809

John Wiley & Sons (Canada) Ltd, 22 Worcester Road,
Rexdale, Ontario M9W 1L1, Canada

Library of Congress Cataloging-in-Publication Data

Masson, J. M. (Judith M.)
    Out of hearing : representing children in care proceedings / Judith Masson and Maureen Winn Oakley.
        p.   cm. — (Wiley series in child protection and policy)
    Includes bibliographical references and index.
    ISBN 0-471-98642-9 (alk. paper)
    1. Custody of children—United States.   2. Child abuse—Law and legislation—United States.   3. Children—Legal status, laws, etc.—United States.   4. Children as witnesses—United States.   5. Legal assistance to children—United States.   I. Winn Oakley, Maureen. II. Title.   III. Series: NSPCC/Wiley child protection and policy series.
KF547.M375   1999
346.7301'73—dc21   98-35141
                                                          CIP

British Library Cataloguing in Publication Data

A catalogue record for this book is available from the British Library

ISBN 0-471-98642-9

Typeset in 10/12pt Palatino by Dorwyn Ltd, Rowlands Castle, Hants
Printed and bound in Great Britain by Redwood Ltd, Trowbridge
This book is printed on acid-free paper responsibly manufactured from sustainable forestry, in which at least two trees are planted for each one used for paper production.

CONTENTS

For our children:
Leo and Amy,
Tom and Em.

. . . who remind us to listen.

ABOUT THE AUTHORS

Judith Masson is a Professor of Law at Warwick University, specialising in child law and teaching law students, social workers and doctors. She is joint author with Dr Stephen Cretney of *Principles of Family Law* (6th edn, 1997) Sweet and Maxwell and with Michael Morris of the *Children Act Manual* (1992) Sweet and Maxwell. She has been involved in the field of socio-legal research in family and child law for many years, conducting studies on adoption by parent and step-parent, *Mine, Yours or Ours?* (1983) HMSO; the use of wardship by local authorities; kinship and inheritance, J. Finch et al, *Wills, Inheritance and Families* (1996) OUP; and social work partnerships with parents of children in long-term care, *Working with Children and 'Lost' Parents* (1997) YPS. She is currently researching children's civil litigation and legal aid for the Lord Chancellor's Department.

Maureen Winn Oakley is NSPCC Research Fellow at the School of Law, University of Warwick. She was coordinator of the Kidderminster Women's Aid Refuge prior to completing her PhD on Domestic Violence. She went on to train as a family law solicitor. She has been involved in research on the Children Act 1989 for some years, working for Bristol University, at both the Socio-Legal Centre and the National Council for Family Proceedings. She is presently engaged in research involving Independent Visitors and Advocacy Services and will shortly start a new project, with Judith Masson, on police and emergency protection.

PREFACE

In 1995 the National Society for the Prevention of Cruelty to Children (NSPCC) established a fellowship at Warwick University to undertake research on representing children. This followed on from the NSPCC national campaign aimed at parents and those providing services to children about the importance of listening to children. Chris Brown, the then Director and Chief Executive of the NSPCC, stated, 'If we are to serve children effectively we must be prepared to listen and learn from what children have to say to us.' Researchers were becoming more aware of the absence of children's voices from narratives about their lives, the invisibility of children in official statistics and the lack of knowledge of children's perceptions amongst policy makers and service providers in health, education, social services and the legal system. A more collaborative approach to qualitative research was developing. The focus became research *with* children rather than just *about* them.

Children and young people caught up in proceedings about their care and protection are particularly vulnerable. Their future depends on both the social welfare and the legal systems, as well as their parents and family. Communication between them and these systems is vital. Although there had been research into the court processes in child protection, including the perspectives of the various professionals involved and those of parents, little was known about how children and young people experienced child protection proceedings. We developed this study specifically with the aim of redressing that imbalance by giving a voice to the children and young people involved in such court cases.

We are indebted to the NSPCC for financial support, without which this research could not have been undertaken, and for their encouragement and assistance in completing this project. Special thanks are due to Dr Pat Cawson, whose perceptive comments and positive approach helped us to persevere. We also wish to acknowledge the contribution of our advisory committee: Professor Lee Bridges of Warwick University Legal Research Institute, Katherine Gieve, partner with the Bindmans solicitors, Barbara Joel-Esam, lawyer NSPCC Public Policy Department, Mavis Maclean from the Oxford Centre for Socio-legal Studies, Arran Poyser, social services inspector with the Department of Health, Janet Read from the Department of Applied Social Studies at Warwick University and Kevin Smith, Panel Manager of Leicestershire GALRO panel. Overall, the research could not have taken place without the cooperation of the children and young people who were willing to allow the researchers to observe their meetings with their representatives and to discuss their experiences, and of the guardians ad litem, the solicitors, the panel managers and all the other gatekeepers to the system. We are most grateful for the consideration and time all these people gave to the research. Our final thanks go to Mrs Nihid Iqbal, our research secretary.

This book reflects the views of the authors and does not necessarily reflect or express NSPCC policy.

1

SETTING THE SCENE

'To begin with a cruel paradox: in spite of all the care and concern, the easiest thing to do in child abuse work is to lose the child's perspective – to miss what the experience means to an abused child.'   (Moore 1985)

This book is about the way children and young people are represented in proceedings brought in the civil courts for their protection. It is based on observations of the meetings between 20 children and young people and their representatives, and on interviews with them and their representatives after the proceedings had been completed. The children and young people, six girls and young women and 14 boys and young men, were all aged between 8 and 16 years. The fieldwork was undertaken over approximately 15 months in two areas of the Midlands of England in 1996–7. Further details of the research methods are given in Appendix II.

The research records the experiences and views of the children and young people who participated. It does not claim to be representative of the experiences of all children and young people caught up in these proceedings, nor of the work of their representatives. The majority of children involved are much younger; 40 per cent are under the age of 5 years (DH 1995c), and are consequently less able to understand, to explain or to participate than the children and young people who allowed the researchers to see and hear what it was like for them. But it should be noted that the representatives had between them many years of experience and that many of the guardians ad litem were or had been members of panels in other areas.

Throughout the research and in the analysis the researchers have consciously tried to examine the representation process from the children's and young people's perspectives – what they understood about the process, how involved they felt in it and to what extent their representatives addressed their concerns. Knowledge about representation derived from focusing on children's and young people's views and experiences adds further dimensions to understandings which have depended on the views of adults. Judges, magistrates, solicitors, social workers, guardians ad litem and parents all have their own perspectives about how child protection proceedings operate. These reflect their status as adults and the role they have in the proceedings.

The Children Act 1989 defines all those under the age of 18 years as children, replacing the previous legal terms of minors and infants. The term 'child' can be confusing, referring as it does either to a status and contrasting with majority (adulthood), or to a relationship. Its breadth, from infancy to the verge of adulthood, encompasses a wide range of abilities and needs related to stages of development. It can also be derogatory; childishness is immaturity and someone who is childlike lacks understanding. Young people, those of secondary school age for example, do not talk about themselves as children, they are young people. The researchers have preferred to use the phrase *children and young people* to emphasise their consideration of young people's perspectives and to avoid the impression that all who are being represented have the same needs and wishes as the very young.

Elsewhere the researchers use various technical terms relating to the law and court proceedings. To make the text accessible for those who have less familiarity wth this jargon, these terms are identified and explained in this chapter.

THE LEGAL FRAMEWORK

The Children Act 1989 together with regulations and Court Rules made under it provide the legal framework for England and Wales. Similar provision is made for Northern Ireland in the Children (Northern Ireland) Order 1995; Scottish law is substantially different. The Children Act was the culmination of nearly a decade of debate informed by empirical research, practice experience and enquiries into incidents including the deaths of children in care and the handling of allegations of child sexual abuse. The Act sets out the rights and responsibilities governing the relationships between children, parents and the State, the conditions, standards and procedure for court proceedings about children's upbringing, and the powers of the court to determine disputes or make orders in respect of children. *Private law* proceedings under the Children Act concern only children and families; *public law* cases involve the State, which has a role protecting children and young people. The research concerned representation for children and young people in *public law* proceedings but is relevant to the ongoing debate about whether and how they should be involved in *private law* proceedings, for example where parents are in dispute about their care, or where incidents of domestic violence highlight child protection issues.

Legal responsibility for the protection of children and young people rests with the social services departments of local authorities. Child protection work is only one aspect of social services work with children and families, but it has tended to dominate organisation and thinking in recent years, despite attempts in the Children Act to emphasise work to support families

(DH 1995b). Local authorities have a statutory duty to investigate where there are concerns about child protection, and they can call upon the assistance of other agencies, health trusts, education departments, the police and others. But only local authorities (and the NSPCC) can bring *care proceedings* and seek a *care order or supervision order* to ensure the long-term protection of children from harm within their families.

The Children Act emphasises cooperation between local authorities and parents over the protection of children who are suffering or at risk of significant harm. It empowers local authorities to look after children by agreement with parents and discourages the use of court orders where arrangements can be agreed. Consequently, cases which come before the courts tend to be those where the local authority has been unable to make an agreement with the parents, where agreements have been broken, or the social services department considers that the seriousness of the situation or the action it wishes to take necessitates the authority of a court order. Court proceedings are in many senses a 'last resort' (Hunt and Macleod 1997).

If a child or young person is made the subject of a *supervision order* in care proceedings the local authority is required to advise, assist and befriend the child. The local authority supervises the child's care; parents, carers and the child must comply with the supervisor's directions.

A *care order* gives the local authority parental responsibility for the child which is shared with the parents. The local authority also has responsibility for safeguarding and promoting welfare, accommodating and maintaining the child and the power and responsibility for making and implementing decisions about the child's future. Ninety per cent of children and young people who are subject to care orders are placed away from their family home at some time while the order is in force. In relation to most decisions about children in care, the local authority is required only to consult the parents, the child and others who have relevant views, but a few decisions also require authorisation from the court. Placement in secure accommodation except for very limited periods, arrangements for the child to live abroad, restriction of family contact and the child's adoption all require court approval. In addition, a court order is required to extend a supervision order or to discharge a care or supervision order, but not to place a child at home, with relatives or for adoption.

At any one time local authorities in England and Wales look after 50 000 children and young people, about 60 per cent of whom are the subject of care orders. In 1996, nearly 32 000 children and young people started to be looked after by local authorities, almost 3000 following the making of care orders. A similar number entered under emergency protection orders or police protection; many of these were subsequently made subject to care orders. Half the children and young people entering the care system, but less than a quarter entering as a result of court proceedings, were over the age of 10 years. During the same year 4000 children and young people who had been subject to care orders ceased to be looked after by a local authority; for nearly half, their care order was not discharged but expired because they reached the age of 18 years.

In 1996 over 16 000 *public law* Children Act proceedings were started. These included over 5000 applications for care orders, 1300 applications for supervision orders, 1100 applications for secure accommodation orders, 800 applications for the discharge of care orders and 2700 applications relating to contact (Judicial Statistics 1996, 51). The majority of these applications result in the making of the order requested, a few applications are refused and some are withdrawn. The court may make a different order, for example a supervision order on an application for a care order, and vice versa. If it does not make a care order the court can make a *residence order* to settle the arrangements for the child's care. This confirms that a child is to live with an individual, for example a parent or relative and gives them parental responsibility if they do not already have it.

The Children Act established a system of triple jurisdiction where the three levels of court, family proceedings court, county court and the High Court, generally have the same powers and operate under comparable Court Rules. The majority of public law cases are heard by lay magistrates in the local family proceedings court but complex cases, particularly those where the final hearing is expected to last three or more days, are transferred to the county court or, more rarely to the High Court, and heard by specialist, professional judges. Approximately one-sixth of *public law* cases are heard in the higher courts.

REPRESENTATION IN COURT PROCEEDINGS

The following case example illustrates what happens to a young person when a local authority decides to bring concerns about their care to court. It outlines key elements in the process, the technical terms used and introduces the professionals who become involved.

> The social services department has been concerned about Kim for some time. Both professionals and relatives have contacted them about his situation, suggesting that he is being neglected and ill treated at home. Over the last few months social workers have tried to improve the care provided by Kim's parents but have had little cooperation. After a series of incidents and injuries and following a discussion with professionals from other agencies, a decision has been made to start care proceedings in the local court. The social services department is not yet sure what Kim will need in the long term. It is bringing proceedings with a view to monitoring and supporting Kim's care at home under a care or supervision order or to removing him and placing him elsewhere.

Kim is likely to experience uncertainty and changes, both before and after proceedings are started. This is in addition to all the feelings he has as a result of being abused and neglected. He may be moved from home to live with local authority approved foster carers whom he does not know or to a children's home, possibly with very little notice. Inevitably this will involve a change in routine and less contact with those he knows. He may also have to change school. He may have to move more than once before the proceedings are concluded; each move involves more changes. If Kim does not already have a local authority social worker he should be allocated one to take responsibility for his overall care, arrange assessments of him and, with other social workers, prepare the plans for his future care. All these arrangements are likely to bring Kim into contact with other professionals, doctors for medical examinations and specialist social workers, psychologists or child psychiatrists for assessments. If there is a criminal investigation because of his ill-treatment he will also be interviewed by police officers.

Within the local authority three interrelated strands of work have to be undertaken: the preparation of the legal case for Kim's future protection, the arrangements for his current care and the assessment and planning for his future care. On the legal side, a solicitor acting for the local authority will need to discuss the case with members of the social work team and identify its basis and merits and file the application to court. Throughout the proceedings further work will need to be undertaken, attending *directions hearings* (where the court makes preliminary decisions about the filing of evidence, assessments and care of Kim and the conduct of the final hearing), making or opposing applications and identifying witnesses and preparing statements for the court. There will also be continuous liaison with the social workers, any expert witnesses and the solicitors for the other *parties* to the proceedings. If Kim is being looked after by the local authority, his social worker is required to visit him, monitor the care he is receiving and prepare for regular statutory reviews. The social worker will also be involved in arranging any assessments for Kim or his parents and facilitating contact visits. If Kim has to move or to change school, the social worker will have to arrange this as well. Planning for Kim's future will involve obtaining assessments, discussing potential placements and making a case for allocation of the resources to pay for it.

Kim's parents may have been invited to and attended a local authority *case conference*, a meeting of the professionals who have knowledge relevant to planning Kim's care, and expect action to be taken. Alternatively, the realisation that the local authority intended to bring proceedings may have been unanticipated by them. They are likely to experience a number of conflicting emotions, particularly if Kim is removed: confusion, anger, resentment, relief, guilt and anxiety. The allegations and recriminations may strain their relationship to breaking point. They need legal advice and may be uncertain about how to get this. They may not be aware of specialist lawyers, or that they will qualify for legal aid. The proceedings place further demands on them to respond to the local authority and put forward a case to counter that of the professionals.

The court must decide whether the local authority has established that Kim is suffering or likely to suffer *significant harm* (Children Act 1989, s. 31) and what order, if any, should be made in Kim's best interests. The proceedings will probably take at least six months. During this time there will be other decisions for the court. These may include: should an *interim care order* be made allowing Kim's removal from home before the final hearing? If so, should any particular arrangements for *contact* with his parents or others be ordered? What assessments should be undertaken of Kim and of his parents? Should evidence be sought from experts, and if so, from whom? When and where will the final decision be taken?

What is Kim's part in the dispute between his parents and the social services department? How does the court know what is in Kim's interests? To what extent are Kim's own views considered?

When the local authority brings these proceedings or other *specified proceedings*, including applications for secure accommodation or contact orders, or when parents seek the discharge of a care order or contact with a child in care, the children and young people concerned are named as *parties* to those proceedings. The court is required to appoint a *guardian ad litem* to represent them from the local panel of guardians ad litem and reporting officers, unless it is satisfied that it is not necessary to do so. Guardians ad litem are also appointed in contested adoption proceedings even though the child is not a party. Reporting officers witness the parents' agreement to adoption.

The duty to provide a guardian ad litem service for the courts is placed on the local authority. Most authorities do this by employing guardians or appointing them to a panel which they manage themselves, but there are a few panels, including the largest, the Inner and North London Panel, which are managed by voluntary organisations. The independence of the service is protected by the requirement to appoint a panel committee with advisory functions, the absence of any power in the local authority to direct the work of guardians and the disqualification as guardian in any particular case of a person who has been concerned in making arrangements for the child's care in the previous five years. Nevertheless, there have been concerns from professionals and families about the independence of the service (Murch and Hooper 1992, 73). In 1995 there were approximately 1000 guardians ad litem in England providing a service to the courts through 54 separate guardian ad litem and reporting officer (GALRO) panels (DH 1995c).

The guardian, usually a qualified social worker, independent of the local authority, is appointed to represent and advise the child or young person, to investigate the circumstances of the case, to advise the court on the options available to it and to prepare a report. These duties of the guardian ad litem are set out in the Family Proceedings Rules 1991 (FPR r. 4.11). In undertaking all these tasks, the guardian must have regard to the welfare of the child. The guardian ad litem is required to appoint a solicitor for the child. The costs of the child's legal representation is met by legal aid, providing the Legal Aid Board is satisfied that they are reasonably incurred. The solicitor applies for a legal aid certificate which is issued in the child's name.

The solicitor, who is usually a member of the Law Society's specialist Children Panel, provides legal advice, serves and accepts documents on behalf of the child and conducts the child's case in court. The solicitor is required to take instructions from the guardian ad litem unless the child is competent to give instructions, wishes to do so and is in conflict with the guardian. In such cases the solicitor must take instructions from the child; a guardian who wants legal representation has to appoint another solicitor (FPR r. 4.12).

In 1994–5 there were 12 500 requests for guardians ad litem or reporting officer appointments, just over a third of these related to adoption proceedings. Guardians ad litem and reporting officers represented over 18 000 children, three-quarters of whom were below the age of 10 years (DH 1995c).

The *tandem* system of representation by professional, social work guardian ad litem and solicitor differs markedly from the systems provided for children in other civil proceedings in England and Wales. It has been claimed that it is 'one of the most comprehensive and sophisticated operating in any country' and provides 'a neat and effective working synthesis of rights and welfare, which ensures that courts are given the maximum information and opportunity to make proper and wise decisions in respect of children' (Timms 1995, 81–82).

The following chapter outlines the theoretical and legal background to provision of representation for children and young people. The rest of the book focuses on the agendas of the young people involved in the proceedings, of the system and of the representatives. The final chapter discusses the policy and practice implications of the research findings.

2

RIGHTS, REPRESENTATION AND REPRESENTATIVES

Children and young people, those under the age of majority, have a special status which is reflected in their legal and social position in all communities. Lesser power and status is accorded to those who are not adults. To be a child is to lack the full legal capacity of adults, the right to make decisions for oneself, to own land, to vote and to do many other things which adults take for granted. Children's views are not accorded the same respect as those of adults, whatever their age or experience, and children and young people are not regarded as experts in their own lives. Children are under the protection of parents and the State; parents and the State control children's lives, expanding or limiting their opportunities.

Children and young people are denied or relieved of the responsibilities of adulthood because they cannot be expected to cope with them or because they need to be protected from them. The notions of incapacity and protection are bound together; protection is required because children's more limited capacity means that they cannot physically or emotionally protect themselves. Holding children to be incapable is also a means of protecting them from the dangers of the adult world and from themselves. Children who are denied the power to make decisions are not allowed to harm themselves. But protecting children from making mistakes denies them the opportunity to learn by experience, encourages dependence and reinforces incompetence.

The law's construction of children as lacking capacity is not simply a matter of their protection. Children are subject to the control of parents and others who are in the position of parents. Relationships between the State and the family have been based on the notion of family privacy, the right of the family, meaning parents or even fathers, to determine how family life is conducted free from State interference. Family privacy was accepted because it furthered the State's interests and freed it from responsibility for children's wellbeing (O'Donovan 1993, 24). Protecting children from harm in the family necessitates reducing the power of parents and the acceptance of responsibility by the State. Although child protection may now be seen as a recognition of children's rights it was originally based on paternalism, the moral obligation to rescue, and concerns that neglected children would threaten good order in society.

CHILDREN, YOUNG PEOPLE AND THEIR RIGHTS

Despite the limitations of childhood there is now worldwide acceptance of the notion that children have rights. The Universal Declaration of Human Rights and the various regional human rights conventions such as the European Convention on Human Rights make no exception for children. Children have the rights to life and liberty, to free speech and fair hearing, and to family life because they are guaranteed to all. The UN Convention on the Rights of the Child goes further by identifying rights which recognise the special character of childhood and the particular interests of children and young people. Moreover, this Convention has been ratified by over 190 countries in less than 10 years, making it the most successful Convention in the history of the United Nations. Despite this near-universal acceptance, the concept and implications of children having rights, the question of what rights children should and do have, and the practice of ensuring rights for children all remain highly problematic.

Rights for children and young people

The phrase *children's rights* is commonly used in different ways reflecting both moral and legal entitlements. Identifying something as *a right* appears to give it a higher status than other claims but construction as a right depends on there being an obligation on somebody to fulfil it. To say that children have the right to be loved by their parents is quite different from saying that young people have a right to adequate care from their parents. There is only a *moral* duty to love, no legal action can be taken because a parent fails to love their child. But if a young person is not given adequate care, the parents may be prosecuted for neglect or the young person may be removed for their protection. Child welfare services exist to ensure that families have support for their caring role and that children and young people are not ill-treated. The right to be cared for is reflected in enforceable obligations on the parents and on the State. In this case, enforcement is not by the young person; the young remain ultimately dependent for their rights on the State's law enforcement or child welfare services.

Children's incapacity poses problems for their recognition as right holders. It has been suggested that children would be better served by imposing obligations (O'Neill 1992) but the notion of fundamental obligations does not have the status and power of fundamental rights. Young children do not have the autonomy on which the 'will' theory depends (MacCormick 1976). However, the 'interest' theory, which recognises rights based on an identifiable interest and a corresponding duty, has been widely relied upon as the basis for children's rights. The emphasis on responsibilities as a justification for having rights has also undermined the case for recognising that children have rights (Lansdown 1995, 28).

The UN Convention on the Rights of the Child does not provide for enforcement by or on behalf of individual children. Ratifying States agree to provide the Convention rights or, in the case of economic and social rights, to implement them to the extent that their economic situation allows. States are expected to develop their own legal and administrative mechanisms to enable children to receive their rights. The Convention relies on political not legal methods of enforcement; States must report to the Committee on the Rights of the Child on their progress in implementing the Convention. However, some States, but not the United Kingdom, have incorporated the Convention into their constitutions so that it is applied in their courts and individuals may base claims on the rights guaranteed in it.

The implications of recognising that children and young people have rights depend on what rights they are guaranteed. The law has traditionally regarded the family as a private sphere and left unregulated relationships within families. Under the common law children were subject to the control of their father and had no legal rights against him. Allowing children rights against their parents necessarily changes the balance of relationships within the family. The fact that children's rights may need to be protected or enforced by others on their behalf means that relationships which were previously considered private have to be open to outside scrutiny. If children and young people are entitled to something, they are no longer subject to absolute adult control but their limitations may still leave them to depend on adults to receive their rights.

Bainham has asked rhetorically if it matters whether the protection of children's interests is based on their rights or their welfare (Bainham 1993, 81). He acknowledges that terminology may have a symbolic and educative effect on social attitudes but emphasises that it is the substance of relationships rather than the theoretical descriptions applied to them which have the greatest effect.

Substance is clearly important but rights do make a difference. Many things have been done for and with children on the basis of their welfare which could not be justified by reference to their rights. Children from Britain were sent to distant parts of the Commonwealth and denied knowledge of their families (Bean and Melville 1989); in Australia and the United States children were taken from indigenous communities and placed in institutions and throughout Europe and North America children lost their identities through institutionalization and adoption (Masson and Harrison

1996). The concepts of welfare and needs have allowed adults, individually or as organisations, to determine what should be provided for children on the basis of their personal beliefs, and often without reference to children and young people themselves. For example, long after corporal punishment had been made illegal in relation to adults it was still possible for some parents, carers and professionals to suggest that a child 'needed a good thrashing'. Recognising children's rights checks adult power, particularly the power of professionals who can claim to have special insights on welfare or needs. Where services have been based on professional assessments of needs or welfare, the recognition of rights may require a change of priorities.

Which rights?

Once the notion of children's rights is accepted as a powerful basis on which claims can be founded, there is a danger that it will be used not to further the interests of children and young people but as a way adults can pursue their interests. For example, it has been said that children have a 'right' to contact with both their parents after parental separation. This right is the basis of the contact order (Children Act 1989, s. 8), which requires the person with care to allow the child to visit the person named in the order. But a child who wishes to maintain contact with the absent parent has no way of enforcing this against the wishes of that parent; the 'right' of the child is, in reality a right of the absent parent to choose whether or not to maintain contact.

Eekelaar's work on the emergence of children's rights provides a basis for identifying children's rights which reflect their interests and not merely those of adults. He has shown that it is possible to identify independent interests which children might plausibly claim and on which their rights could be based. He argued that children have a 'basic' interest in receiving the essentials for healthy living, a 'developmental' interest in having an equal opportunity to maximise their potential and an 'autonomy interest' in exercising choice on matters of lifestyle and social relations. The 'autonomy interest' may conflict with the basic interest; children may lose the opportunity to become rational adults if they are not subject to some protective control. For this reason Eekelaar ranks this interest subordinate to the other two (Eekelaar 1986).

The potential for conflict between protective rights and rights to self-determination is a central concern in the recognition of children's rights. Although it has been argued that children should have the same rights as adults (Holt 1975; Farson 1978), children's dependence and immaturity has generally been accepted as necessitating greater protection and less autonomy. However, broad acceptance of protection as a basis for children's right may leave no room for autonomy. Freeman has argued for a middle way which acknowledges both autonomy and protection. Whereas protective rights should be available to all, autonomy rights should depend on an individual assessment of a young person's capacity (Freeman 1983). At the theoretical level this appears to provide the necessary balance. In practice, there is a danger that those who wish to control children will be able to ensure that issues or processes remain very complex in order to justify the denial that young people have the capacity necessary for autonomy.

The rights recognised in the UN Convention on the Rights of the Child are based not only on these theoretical concerns but also on agreement about what rights are important to children and young people. It was the intention of those promoting the idea of the Convention that it should reflect what was important to and for children, and have wide international support. The delegates from States, children's organisations and human rights organisations had to take account of the different experiences of children in different communities so as to ensure that the rights in the Convention were relevant to them. The Convention has been very successful in achieving these aims and now provides a definitive list of the rights the international community believes children and young people should have.

Delivering rights

If children and young people are to be able to exercise their rights they must have information about what their rights are. But information is not enough; children and young people may not be able to understand what their rights are nor recognise the relevance of their rights to their situation. Childhood is an enclosed world, physically, socially and emotionally. Young people are not free to seek information and gain knowledge but depend on adults to enable them to identify possibilities and explore opportunities. If rights are to make a difference to their lives, children and young people cannot be left to claim their rights.

The delivering of rights to children and young people demands the development of new processes. Children and young people have an interest in being able to influence decisions about themselves; participation is crucial to the way decisions are received. Professionals who think they know children's wishes have often misunderstood what they want and, in consequence, proposed inappropriate action (Butler and Williamson 1994). According to Eekelaar, 'Hearing what children say must lie at the root of any deliberation on children's rights.' Even where the child is too young to voice an opinion, rights-based decision-making 'stipulates a process which requires serious attention to be given to what the child in question is likely to have wanted if fully informed and mature' (Eekelaar 1992, 229). The focus on the child not only provides the prospect of objectively better decisions, taking account of the individual child but demands a process through which the decision can be justified in terms of what is known about the child.

So long as adults remain central to any process, it is crucial that all adults involved in ensuring children receive a rights-based service, value and respect children's rights. Paternalism has to be kept to a minimum and carefully justified (Fortin 1998, 28). There will always be a need for some external checks that action justified on the basis of children's rights or children's wishes truly reflects these. Where the child's welfare is claimed as the basis for a decision, the advantages to the child should be tested against those of the decision-maker and the system.

RIGHTS TO REPRESENTATION

Article 12 of the UN Convention on the Rights of the Child states:

'1. States Parties shall assure to the child who is capable of forming his or her own views the right to express those views freely in all matters affecting the child, the views of the child being given due weight in accordance with the age and maturity of the child.
2. For this purpose, the child shall in particular be provided with the opportunity to be heard in any judicial and administrative proceedings affecting the child, either directly or through a representative or an appropriate body, in a manner consistent with the procedural rules of national law.'

The Convention does not give a right to representation but requires children to be provided with the opportunity to have their views heard in proceedings about them. The rights to express views and to be heard are not to be limited to those with mature views; any child who is capable of forming a view has the right to express it. All views must be considered, age and maturity are only relevant to determining the weight to be accorded to the child's views. The Convention expresses no preference between direct opportunities to participate, representation and transmission of the child's views in other ways, for example by a welfare officer. But those charged with reporting the child's views must be appropriate; arguably organisations with obligations to make recommendations about welfare are insufficiently independent for this task. Although the views of children and young people may be decisive, the best interests of the child shall be a primary consideration (art. 3(1)).

The Council of Europe welcomed the adoption of the UN Convention of the Rights of the Child and recognised the need for further action to implement it. The European Convention on the Exercise of Children's Rights opened for signature in January 1996 and has yet to be ratified by the United

Kingdom. The Convention seeks to supplement the UN Convention by providing a framework for the implementation of children's rights in legal
proceedings. It focuses on family proceedings; States ratifiying the Convention are required to identify three categories of family proceedings to which
they will apply the Convention, for example residence, contact, care proceedings and adoption, and decide how best to do this within their national
law. Children do not have to be given party status in the chosen proceedings
but, under article 3, children who have sufficient understanding shall be
granted and shall be entitled to request the following rights:

(a) To receive all relevant information.
(b) To be consulted and express his or her views.
(c) To be informed of the possible consequences of compliance with these
    views and the possible consequences of any decision.

Relevant information is information which is appropriate to the age and
understanding of the child, given to enable the child to exercise his or her
rights fully 'unless the provision of such information were contrary to the
welfare of the child' (art. 2d). These rights are to be protected through
obligations on the courts and on representatives, but do not apply where
this would be 'manifestly contrary' to the best interests of the child. The
courts must ensure that children have the necessary information and opportunities to express their views either directly or through individuals or agencies. They must give due weight to these views. Representatives, who may
be individual lawyers, welfare officers or organisations, must provide information and explanations (arts 6 and 10). Children will also be entitled to
apply for a 'special representative' where conflict of interest between themselves and those who have parental responsibilities precludes representation by parents (arts 4 and 9). Where legal aid or advice is available for
children's representation it should also cover special representatives (art.
14).
    In this way the Convention seeks both to recognise the importance of
parents in protecting and promoting children's rights and to ensure that the
State plays an active role. Also, to enable children to participate in proceedings without harming themselves by so doing. Family privacy remains a
basic principle, rights of participation are only provided where representation by the family is inappropriate, and in family proceedings where the
involvement of the court already breaches it. The best interests of children
and child protection are prominent themes. The Convention rests on the
assumption that promoting children's rights and providing procedural
rights is in children's best interests, but children need not be accorded their
rights of representation where this is manifestly contrary to their best interests. Courts must consider whether they have sufficient information to act in

children's best interests (art. 6a) and must have power to act without any application where the welfare of the child is in serious danger (art. 8).

The United Kingdom has not ratified the European Convention because the current law does not comply with it. Rights to representation within the terms of the Convention are not routinely provided for all children in three of the categories of proceedings identified in the Convention. Representation in care proceedings provides children and young people with many of the rights set out in the Convention but insufficient attention is given in the Court Rules to providing information and explanations. In private law family proceedings, welfare officers may be said to fulfil the role of representative but the majority of children do not see a welfare officer and little attention is given to providing information or explanations as required by the Convention.

Children and young people who are parties to legal proceedings in England and Wales have access to legal aid for representation without reference to their parents' means. The merits of any application and the child's need for legal representation are generally relevant. In 'specified proceedings' all children have rights to representation by a guardian ad litem and a solicitor unless the court considers this to be unnecessary, but in other proceedings their opportunities for participation are far more limited. Thus, in other family proceedings children and young people are not usually parties, although they may be joined as parties where this is thought desirable. However, a welfare report is generally considered by the court to be sufficient. A child or young person who has sufficient understanding may apply for leave to bring proceedings but such involvement is not regarded favourably by the judiciary (Masson 1996, 247) and the application must always be made to the High Court (*President's Direction* 1993). Where they are not parties their views may be communicated to the court by a welfare officer, but welfare officers are involved in only a minority of cases and do not always speak to children separately from their parents. More rarely, children and young people may write or speak to the judge in person. 'The methods whereby children's wishes are conveyed to the court are so inefficient and arbitrary that it is almost a matter of coincidence whether the court receives a clear idea of what these are' (Fortin 1998, 168).

Representation as a right

Representation can be constructed as either a right of protection or as a right of autonomy. Clearly where the representative is required to advocate the child's or young person's best interests, the focus is protection – making sure that the court hears arguments based on an assessment of the child's welfare situation and not only the interests of the other parties. The way the representative establishes what the best interests are is crucial. The representative and the court must be confident that there has been a proper assessment of welfare; if not, the purpose of the representation is undermined; the court may hear another view but it may not be one which promotes the child's or young person's wellbeing. Where the court is required to give paramount consideration to the welfare of the child, there is little room for the lay court to disagree with a properly formulated case from the professional welfare representative. Even a judge who is a specialist in child law must generally defer to the professional assessment of the child's welfare. In these circumstances representation may effectively replace a court evaluation of the issues and be the way the child is protected in the proceedings.

Representation can be seen as a right of protection even where the representative is not required to represent the child's welfare. Being represented makes a difference; arguments for the provision of representation and for the extension of legal aid in civil and criminal proceedings have emphasised the poor outcomes for those who face court proceedings without representation (King 1971; Genn and Genn 1989; Bridges et al 1995, 148). Clients who have a representative are guided through the process; they should be told what to expect and, in the knowledge that their representative will take care of it, they may avoid some of the anxiety of not understanding what is happening.

Representatives' knowledge and experience enables them to be responsive to the court and thus to interpret the client's case in ways which the court will find attractive (Anderson 1978). This protects the client, whether their interests or their wishes are being represented. But the focus on protection may influence the representative to place less emphasis on getting instructions from the client because of beliefs that the client will be best protected by the representative doing what is required.

The representative also stands between the client and the court, protecting the client from the court and the legal process. Representatives' concerns to protect the client from damage may lead them to avoid delving into issues too deeply and from involving the client in the proceedings (King and Young 1992, 1). The fact of representation may allow the court to dispense with or excuse the client's attendance at some or all of the hearings. The court's communication with the client occurs only through the representative, a person known to and often chosen by the client; the representative transmits and translates the client's requests and the court's decisions. In criminal proceedings, attending court as a witness is recognised to be a traumatic event for children, particularly if they will meet the person who is alleged to have committed offences against them. Care is taken to look after child witnesses waiting to give evidence. Elaborate procedures, using closed-Circuit television, have been developed to shield young witnesses from the stress of being in a courtroom or seeing the accused. Representation may also exclude or inhibit the participation of the client (Macleod and Malos 1984). Physical arrangements of the court which separate the client from the representative can create a barrier to communication through the representative. The emphasis on protection may thus conflict with the client's autonomy.

A right to be represented does not imply a right to decide, that is the role of the court, but the provision of representation can empower the client in the process, enabling him or her to direct the case within the limits of the law. If representation is to promote the clients's autonomy, clients must have knowledge about the process and freedom to choose how their case is to be presented. But they may choose not to play an active part and to leave matters in the hands of their representative. Representation aids the client's participation but does not require the client to be more active than he or she wishes. The obligation of the representative to follow the client's instructions means that the client's choice should be respected, but this may leave the representative to put forward an unattractive and ultimately unsuccessful case.

The European Convention on the Exercise of Children's Rights emphasises the 'idea of promoting children's rights' (European Convention 1995). The notion of promotion is broader than that of protection, indicating that children's rights will be developed and that children will be encouraged and assisted to exercise their rights. The main mechanism of the Convention for promoting rights is the provision of representation directed at determining the views of children and young people who have sufficient understanding and presenting them to the court. Specific duties are imposed on representatives to ensure that children have the information and explanations they require in order to form their views unless this would be manifestly contrary to the child's welfare. Thus the Convention seeks to ensure that children have rights to participate in proceedings which concern them and to protect children from the harm of insufficient or inappropriate explanations. This notion of promotion of children's rights combines rights to protection with rights to autonomy by emphasising protection through participation, and by limiting exclusion for protection to cases of obvious harm.

Representation for children

The fact that a child or young person is represented in court proceedings does not guarantee that their views will be strenuously advocated before the court. The methods and goals of the representation depend on the ethical, legal and social context of representation, particularly the representative's relationship with their young client, with other participants and with the court. Representing children is a very delicate, sensitive and time-consuming process (King and Young 1992, 1).

A representative for the child may be appointed as the child's guardian ad litem or the child's lawyer. In some circumstances the lawyer may be expected to fulfil both roles; alternatively, the form of representation may be unclear. Although the terms may be confused and the roles may overlap, there is an essential difference between the two forms of representation for children. Whereas the primary focus of the guardian ad litem is the protection of the child's interests before the court, which may include ensuring that the court is informed about the child's wishes, a lawyer is generally expected to follow the client's instructions. A single person with both roles may experience conflict and be ineffective in either of them; for example, where a child client wants the representative to advocate a position which the representative considers is against the child's interests.

Lawyers for children and young people have long been exercised by the potential for conflict between their client's wishes and their client's interests. Is it ethical for a lawyer to advocate for a course of action favoured by a young client in the knowledge that this would be contrary to their interests? In what circumstances is it appropriate for the child's lawyer to disregard the views of their client? If the lawyer does so, can he or she continue to provide representation? And if so, on what basis? Is there a third way which ethically allows the lawyer to seek to influence the client to put forward views which do not clash with the court's likely perception of their interests? These are real dilemmas: legal obligations and rules for representatives can alleviate but not eliminate them.

Of course it can be argued that the lawyer does not have knowledge about what is in the child's interests, only opinion, which should not influence the relationship with the client. The young client's instructions should therefore be treated like the instructions of any other client. However, such an approach denies the influence previous experiences have on lawyers and treats representation as a mechanical rather than a human process. But taking instructions is a two way process through which the representative helps the client to formulate their goals in the light of knowledge of the court's approach. The lawyer's experience will often give him or her a good indication of how the court will evaluate the alternative courses of action. The young client is not in the same position as an adult; he or she may be more vulnerable to pressure or persuasion.

The relative immaturity of a young client may be taken as justifying not following instructions on the basis that he or she is not competent to give instructions. The assessment of competence is a difficult issue and one on which children's lawyers have expressed differing views (Sawyer 1995). What cannot be denied is the power of the lawyer to contribute to or undermine the client's ability to give coherent instructions. Reasonable instructions, those which accord with the lawyer's (or the court's) perception of what should occur, are more likely to be accepted. The child or young person who wishes to pursue a reckless path can be viewed as expressing their immaturity, and their instructions should not be followed because they are not competent to give them. But refusing to take a young client's instructions may usurp the position of the judge as final arbiter and may ultimately be contrary to the client's welfare interests. The court is denied a crucial perspective and, in consequence, may approve a solution intolerable to the child or young person.

The American Bar Association has proposed standards for lawyers who practise in abuse and neglect cases. It strongly prefers the appointment of the lawyer as a 'child's attorney' with 'the same duties of undivided loyalty, confidentiality, and competent representation' as is due to an adult client (ABA 1995, 376). The child's lawyer should be prepared to participate fully in any proceedings and not merely defer to the other parties. He or she should elicit the child's preferences in a way appropriate for the child's stage of development and represent them, following the child's directions throughout the proceedings.

The commentary on the American Bar Association proposals focuses on the importance of the lawyer's relationship with the child as an instrument in avoiding conflict between the child's instructions and welfare interests. Although it notes that the lawyer should be careful not to apply 'undue presssure' on a child, it acknowledges that 'the lawyer's advice and guidance can often persuade the child to change an imprudent position or to identify alternative choices' (ABA 1995, 379). Ethical conflict 'can be resolved through the lawyer's counselling function. If the lawyer has taken the time to establish rapport with the child and gain the child's trust, it is likely that the lawyer will be able to persuade the child to abandon a dangerous position' (ABA 1995, 382). If this does not occur, the ABA propose that the lawyer should request the appointment of a guardian ad litem but not reveal the basis for the request because this would compromise the child's position. The child's welfare will then be protected by the guardian ad litem, leaving the lawyer to follow their client's instructions. Moreover, in circumstances where the child is in 'grave danger of serious injury or death, the child's safety must be the paramount concern' (ABA 1995, 383).

Representation of children in proceedings for their protection in England and Wales

Before the introduction of the 'separate representation' provision of the Children Act 1975, the representation of the interests of parents and children in child protection proceedings was conflated. Children, but not parents, were parties to the proceedings with entitlement to legal representation under legal aid, but there was no mechanism for lawyers to obtain instructions from their young clients or guidance about how they should act if they had no instructions. In practice, solicitors generally obtained instructions from the child's parents. The injustice of leaving the parents without representation and the acceptance that children's interests were reflected through their parents justified an approach which could make it difficult for the court to appreciate what the real interests of the child were and have disastrous consequences for the child's right to protection. For example, in one notorious case, the child's lawyers advised the parents to borrow books on child development from the library so that they could impress the social workers about their concern for the child. The lawyer successfully argued for a supervision order rather than a care order, and the child was subsequently re-injured in his home and died (Somerset Area Review Committee 1979).

In 1979 the Law Society issued guidance advising solicitors in receipt of legal aid to represent children that they should not take instructions from parents. Parents had no access to legal aid for representation until 1983, although they could get a limited amount of legal advice and assistance. In 1984, parents became entitled to legal aid in care proceedings but only where the court made an order separating the parents' and the child's interests. When the court made such an order it could also appoint a guardian ad litem for the child. Where the child was not separately represented, the lack of any representation for the parents could mean the court was left without a full presentation of the issues if the child's solicitor did not bring them forward. Representation of the child might therefore still necessitate some presentation of the parents' case. Parents obtained the right to participate in care proceedings as parties with improved legal aid in 1988 but did not get party status until the Children Act 1989 was implemented in 1991.

Lawyers acting for children in care proceedings before the introduction of guardian ad litem reported being unsure about their role. Where they represented younger children they rarely relayed to the court the child's wishes but they might test the local authority's evidence or even seek to lead an alternative view from an independent social worker. In most cases the representative endorsed the local authority's recommendation. There were two approaches to the representation of young people's views – presenting their view with a qualification, or reporting it but arguing that it was contrary to their best interests. Whereas some solicitors obviously provided moral support to children attending the hearing, others appeared to ignore their client (Macleod and Malos 1984).

The introduction of the guardian ad litem system clarified the role of the child's lawyer but until the implementation of the Children Act 1989 there were considerable variations in the appointment of guardians ad litem in care cases and thus in lawyers' access to instructions based on the child's interests. Lawyers generally welcomed the appointment of the guardian ad litem and quickly established good working relationships with them (Murch et al 1989). The solicitor for the child was required by the court rules to follow the guardian ad litem's instructions unless the child wished to give instructions which conflicted with those of the guardian and was competent to do so. Most solicitors were content to follow the guardian's instructions, but a study by Murch and colleagues identified cases where solicitors rejected the guardian's instructions concerning the best interests of young children because they considered that they knew better than the guardian and also cases where solicitors articulated the views of older children but did not argue their case. The lawyers' failure to advocate positions which they considered to be damaging to a young person was 'understandable' but conflicted with 'both the letter and the spirit of the legislation' (Murch et al 1990, 12).

Whilst maintaining the basic division, the Children Act further clarified the roles of guardian ad litem and the solicitor for a child in specified proceedings. The guardian ad litem is required to appoint a solicitor for the child, to instruct the solicitor unless the child is giving instructions and to advise the court of the child's wishes (FPR r. 4.11(2),(4)(b)). Where the child is instructing the solicitor direct or intends to do so, the guardian must inform the court but continues to take such part in the proceedings as the court directs. The court can direct legal representation for the guardian so that the child's interests continue to be advocated (r. 4.11(3)). The solicitor is required to represent the child:

> 'in accordance with instructions received from the guardian ad litem (unless the solicitor considers, having taken into account the views of the guardian ad litem and any directions of the court under rule 4.4.11(3), that the child wishes to give instructions which conflict with those of the guardian ad litem and that he is able, having regard to his understanding, to give such instructions on his own behalf in which case he shall conduct the proceedings in accordance with instructions received from the child)' (r. 4.12(1)(a)).

If there are no instructions from a guardian ad litem or from the child, the solicitor must conduct the case in furtherance of the child's best interests (FPR r. 4.12(1)). Thus, in specified proceedings, the legal representative is required to advocate the child's interests except where the child is permitted to give instructions. The system of tandem representation should enable the court to hear both the child's interests and his or her wishes.

THE CONTEXT OF REPRESENTATION

Whatever the formal rights to representation, its effectiveness is dependent on the context in which it is exercised. Representation encompasses not only advocacy, the presentation of the client's case to the court, but also the identification and investigation of issues from which the case can be constructed, negotiation with other parties to establish areas of agreement and conflict, and advice to the client about the process and its possible outcomes. Different representatives may focus on some of these aspects according to their strengths, the nature of the proceedings, and the client, thereby creating a variety of interactions with the client and the court, all of which could be termed representation. Representation is what representatives do but the actions of representatives cannot simply be viewed as the product of the representatives' professional relationship with an individual with a problem. Representation is shaped by the context in which it is provided and the role it performs in the court process.

There are two distinct paradigms of representation: representation as a service to the person being represented and representation to oil the machinery of justice. The traditional model used by lawyers emphasises the former; lawyers are consulted by clients and give advice which the client accepts or rejects in deciding how to deal with the problem. This ideal of lawyers is valued by children who see 'the helpful solicitor' as someone who, 'defends you against the vagaries of the adult professional world' (Farnfield and Kaszap 1998). The lawyer follows the client's instructions, a process which suggests detachment but which necessarily involves helping the client to understand how the case is viewed in law, what choices there are and how to decide between them.

The functioning of court proceedings in an adversarial system is largely dependent on the representatives. Judges and magistrates rely on representatives to prepare bundles of documents in a way which enables them to get a grasp on the issues and to put the case before them succinctly. 'The efficient preparation of court bundles is an essential element in the art of advocacy.' (B. v. B. 1994, Wall J.) Where there are a succession of hearings before different judges, as commonly occurs in proceedings under the Children Act, the person hearing a particular issue frequently depends on the representatives for an understanding of how it fits into the case as a whole.

Court staff acknowledge that representation oils the wheels of the justice system, it enables them to avoid advising those involved in proceedings so that justice is seen to be done and makes it easier to cope with large case loads by speeding cases through the system. Representatives manage their clients, sharing a goal with court officials to avoid 'the dreaded performance' – open hostility from a parent overcome by the tension of the situation (Parker, Casburn and Turnbull 1981). Children have also identified this aspect of their representation, seeing their representative as their ally but also as an aid to the court (Cashmore and Bussey 1994, 325). Timms suggests that guardians ad litem are also used to facilitate the court proceedings, not just because courts have come to rely on their advice, direction and final recommendation, but in the process and conduct of the case (Timms 1995, 200).

In practice, solicitors may try to operate a combined approach, to aid the client's resolution of their problems by facilitating the process within which the client is caught. Such activity can be presented as furthering the client's interests; the client is more likely to achieve an outcome closest to the one they seek if the case is presented in a way which is attractive to the court. But the demands of the client may conflict with those of the court, for example where the client wants to participate directly and the court prefers to deal only with the lawyer. Similarly, Timms has argued that guardians can be both an officer of the court with responsibilities for case management and an independent representative of the child: 'Effective case management necessarily brings guardians closer to the court, but should not distance them from the child.' (Timms 1995, 201)

Empirical evidence suggests that, at least in criminal proceedings, lawyers get co-opted to work for the court rather than for their client. There are a number of reasons for this; not least is the importance to lawyers of managing their relationships with the other participants so as to maintain their careers. Clients were seen as secondary to a system within which the lawyer has greater professional, economic, intellectual and other ties (Blumberg 1967). In other areas of practice lawyers perform transformations of the client's grievance. These include advising clients about aspects they had not considered and helping clients to decide what their goals are, but lawyers 'often shape disputes to fit their own interests'. They may actively discourage clients from pressing legitimate claims or providing only minimal assistance so that the client is unable to take the issue forward (Felstiner et al 1981). Lawyers and clients have different agendas which they seek to resolve through their interactions (Sarat and Felstiner 1986).

Representation is shaped by the proceedings in which it occurs. An obvious factor is the issues which the court is required to consider. Narrow issues such as status or the effects of a court order restrict the arguments which are relevant whereas broad ones, such as welfare, can justify a more expansive approach. Severe limits on what the representative can argue can produce defeatism, discouraging any activity. Limited representation may also result from pressure to complete a large number of cases within a short period.

The court process is highly relevant. Rights of audience for solicitors enable the person who has had direct dealings with the client in the preparation of the case to present it to the court rather than instructing counsel. Liberal rules about, for example, the admission of hearsay evidence allow the representative choice about how a point is to be put before the court. In cases concerning the care of children, the representative can theoretically choose between presenting their client's experiences to the court through their direct evidence, the evidence of others to whom the client has spoken or a welfare report. The availability of representation to other parties is also an influence. Thus, before the introduction of representation for parents in care proceedings, solicitors for children felt they should ensure that the court was aware of the parents' views (Macleod and Malos 1984).

These are not just matters of Court Rules but also of the accepted practice or ethos of the court. Thus solicitors may appear in care cases in the High Court but local authorities relying on solicitors rather than barristers have been subject to criticism from the judiciary (*Re B.* 1996). Similarly, children may give evidence but the civil courts do not welcome child witnesses; presenting testimony from the child may undermine the representative's credibility and, in consequence, the strength of the argument.

Ethics are also important. How is the representative expected to behave towards the client and the court. This is not only a matter of the rules of professional practice but also about the culture of the court. The flexibility of ethical standards may assist the representative to remain within them but a claim that something is not ethical is easily undermined when other representatives appear to find it acceptable. The representative has to balance two sets of duties which may compete: the duty to the court to conduct the case according to the required standards, for example not to put forward arguments which are known to have no merit, and the duty to the client to follow instructions unless the rules demand otherwise. A representative who cannot legitimately follow the client's instructions must withdraw if he or she cannot persuade the client to a different course. Communication between the representative and the court may therefore be designed to be heard differently by the court and the client and thus to satisfy the demands of both. 'My instructions are' prefaces an argument recognised as weak, alerting the court whilst reassuring the client that the point has been made.

Representation is also shaped by the way it is organised. This is clearly the case in criminal proceedings where the lack of continuous representation of the defendant by an individual and the lack of provision of records of earlier interviews to subsequent representatives both results from and leads to an emphasis on the presentation of the case in court rather than its preparation and investigation (McConville et al 1994). In contrast, a solicitor who is a member of the Law Society Children Panel, representing a child under the Children Act, must give an undertaking to deal with preparation, supervision, conduct and presentation of the case personally. The tandem system of representation in specified proceedings, particularly the appointment of the child's solicitor by the guardian ad litem and the requirement that the solicitor accepts the guardian's instruction except in narrowly defined circumstances, are important factors in determining the representation provided for children. Representation is professional, specialist and personal. But the legal representative's appointment is dependent on his or her selection by the guardian ad litem. It is therefore essential for solicitors to develop and maintain good working relationships with guardians.

The representative's relationship with the person he or she is representing is crucial. A poor relationship may mean that the client is unwilling to confide in their representative who in turn is left without adequate instructions. Where the client can choose who acts as representative and is able to develop a relationship with him or her over a prolonged period, the client has an opportunity to build up trust and knowledge of the representative. In contrast, where representation is provided through a 'duty solicitor' or other assigned representative the relationship may start with limited trust and without the time to develop it. In a study of an Australian system for representing children in care proceedings by duty solicitors, almost half the children and young people interviewed indicated lack of trust for their lawyer and an unwillingness to impart information about themselves. The lawyers also noted their difficulties in establishing a relationship and communicating with their child clients in a single interview (Cashmore and Bussey 1994, 327–329).

Those with experience of a system, repeat players, are generally far more successful in using it than those without (Galanter 1974). The relative weakness of particularly lay clients and the different approach to representing them compared with professional clients who would offer 'repeat business' was noted by Cain. The majority of the lawyers in her detailed study did not seek to control their clients, rather they accepted their clients' objectives, and worked to deliver them. There were, however, a substantial minority of clients who did not receive this service; these were low status clients whose lawyers had conflicting agendas, such as the wish to maintain or develop a patron (Cain 1979).

Within this context it is unrealistic to expect lawyers representing children and young people to remain uninfluenced by the expectations of the court and their professional relationship with the guardian ad litem. The young have low status in the community, those who are involved in care proceedings arguably have even lower status than their peers. Their dual status as children and as victims reinforces the notion that they need protection and control. Children and young people involved in these proceedings lack knowledge and experience of using lawyers or being involved in proceedings, consequently they have great difficulty in influencing the representation provided to them. A lawyer prioritising their professional relationship with their young client over that with the guardian ad litem is acting contrary to the expectations of the system and their own interests. This will be particularly true where the young person's maturity is contestable because of their age, intellectual ability or experiences, and where their instructions clearly contradict accepted understandings about their wellbeing. In many cases the opposition of the guardian ad litem, the court's adviser on the best interests of the child, means that such representation is bound to be unsuccessful. Influencing the young client to accept the guardian's proposal, or some compromise, may be a more successful course of action for the lawyer and for the young person.

3

CHILDREN'S AND YOUNG PEOPLE'S AGENDAS

Children's and young people's agendas were identified through the researcher's observations of the children and young people interacting with their representatives, the guardian ad litem and the solicitor, and through the research interviews. Agendas were defined as being issues which were raised by the children. The agendas reflect the fact that young people were meeting with professionals because of the current court proceedings about their future care. They concerned issues such as attendance at the court hearing and their wishes for the future. Not all issues related directly to the proceedings; children and young people had other preoccupations, and the court proceedings were only one aspect of their daily lives.

The researchers discussed compartmentalising the children's and young people's agendas into issues that appeared to have legal significance and those that did not, but rejected this approach. Adopting such a division might suggest that legal issues were necessarily more important. In effect, children's and young people's agendas would be overlaid with an adult's perception of what is believed to be significant to children during the legal process. In research which is child focused, this would contradict the purpose of recording and relating children's and young people's experiences and understandings.

ISOLATION

Physical isolation

One striking feature about many of the children and young people interviewed for the study was their physical isolation. Children were isolated from their families, friends and communities where they had been living. This was the case for eight children involved in applications for care orders, four involved in secure accommodation applications and two for whom the discharge of a care order was sought. In part this reflects the serious nature of the family dysfunctioning in cases where local authorities seek court orders rather than relying on their powers to provide accommodation. But it also reflects the way children are looked after whilst proceedings are pending, the stigma of being an abused child or being in care and the difficulties social workers have in engaging parents in the child protection process.

Young people's isolation arose out of rejection by parents, lack of contact with parents or relatives whom they yearned to see and placements which left them physically and/or emotionally isolated. Ten young people had very limited contact with family members, distance and location contributing to low levels of contact. Seven children found themselves isolated from other siblings and longed to have contact with them. The children in residential placements had been separated from their home area, schools and friends. Even children continuing to attend the same school felt isolated by the proceedings and were unwilling to talk to friends about such issues.

One young person responded with shock at the thought that child protection professionals may have turned up at his school:

'Oh God . . . No I don't think they did . . . I would have preferred them just to come here [home] . . . 'cause the kids would have asked why and questioned me.'

Foster care was also problematic. The shortage of foster homes meant that children's placements were less than ideal. Four of the young people indicated that they had particularly poor relationships with their carers.

Sylvia's foster carer was infirm and in retirement when the local authority coaxed her to be a short-term carer for Sylvia. Sylvia, aged 14, was the only child in the household and the relationship appeared to be conflictual. The foster carer would berate Sylvia in front of the guardian ad litem, the solicitor and the researcher, complaining about her personal habits and accusing Sylvia of lying. Sylvia told the guardian ad litem, solicitor and researcher how she was not happy with her foster carer and wanted to move. She did not like living so far from her extended family. She was pleased that she continued to attend her original school but she had a long journey by taxi.

Guardians were aware that some children were unhappy in their placements but were also aware of limitations.

'. . . but then you have to say to them, I will go back and I will tell the social worker how you feel but I can't make them move you.'

Isolation through uncertainty

Placements were temporary, and at least six children had changed placements during the proceedings. Such uncertainty compounded their feelings of isolation. Similarly children who knew they were to remain in care did not know where they would be living or when they would move.

Alex, aged 9, was the subject of care proceedings. His mother had died some years before and there were some concerns that Alex and his sister were being neglected by his father and stepmother. Alex's sister had already moved to live with an aunt following a residence order made without local authority involvement. Now the local authority had removed Alex and placed him with short-term foster carers under an interim care order. While proceedings were continuing he was moved to his second foster carers. Alex wanted to go and live with his aunt, his sister and his cousins, and the local authority were looking into this.

Peter, aged 10, was under an interim care order. His mother had rejected him and wanted him to be taken into care. His father was unable to offer him a home. He was now in his second placement. Peter had only been at his present foster carers for about six weeks but he felt settled there. He got on well with both his foster carers and with their other foster child.

> 'I'm glad I'm here . . . Better than my other foster parents . . . I've only had one other fostering but I like this better . . . Yes, got my own bedroom . . . I got cupboards and plenty of toys . . . I hope I can stay here . . . I don't know.'

Although Peter had been placed with this foster family short term, his foster carers were local authority approved long-term carers and cared for the other boy on this basis. Peter did not want to leave and the foster carers had expressed a wish to foster him long term. He was happy with his carers and was pleased that he had remained in his local area where he attended the same school and was now having frequent contact with his father. He accepted that contact with his mother was infrequent but was pleased that he was able to have informal contact with her and his siblings, whom he missed, and who remained at home with his mother. He had bumped into them in the street. Peter valued this informal contact. As his guardian acknowledged,

> 'Social workers had a fear that he would bump into her [mother], which he had done, and that would be upsetting for him, but in fact he seemed able to deal with that, and that seemed to make things normal for him in a way. He could see his mum . . . and he didn't have to have a big long contact session with her. And when he got older he would want to have some contact with her.'

Peter did not want to attend the court hearing and was content for his solicitor and guardian ad litem to present his wishes to the court. He wanted to stay with his present foster carers, to continue with the existing contact arrangements, and to remain at his local school, which he enjoyed.

There could also be uncertainties for those young people about to leave care.

Lucy, aged 10, was waiting at what she called her 'foster house' whilst the final hearing was taking place at court. The court was considering an application to discharge her care order in favour of a residence order to her aunt. She had left her local school the day before and was at her foster carers with her suitcase packed. She had a goodbye present wrapped and ready to give her foster carer. Lucy wanted to live with her aunt. She had been told that she would be leaving her foster home.

'I know I am going to move but I don't know when.'

Her guardian ad litem, social worker and foster carer had all told her that she would probably be moving soon but none of them could tell her exactly when because 'the judge' was the person who would make the decision at the final hearing.

On the one hand there was doubt about Lucy moving, and the professionals involved could not tell her for sure. On the other hand there was ample evidence that a move was imminent. Lucy had finished attending the local school, her foster carer had helped her to pack her suitcase and an adult neighbour interrupted the research interview to say goodbye to Lucy. Lucy was anxiously awaiting to hear the outcome of the court hearing.

Isolation through lack of social worker support

Sylvia, Tom and Carl said that they did not get on with their social workers and felt they could not confide in him or her. This in turn led to feelings of isolation. Carl, aged 11, did not have any confidence in his social worker. He had not wanted to be rehabilitated back home with his mother, and had felt pushed into it by his social worker. Guardians ad litem and solicitors often became aware that some children did not relate to their social workers.

'I think he had quite a lot of faith in me, perhaps because he didn't have any in the social worker.'

Failure to relate to a social worker could increase children's feelings of isolation. So too could the loss of a valued social worker. There were four instances of cases being reallocated during the proceedings where children had lost a social worker they felt had supported them and to whom they could relate.

Martin's social worker was promoted and left the area. Martin, aged 14, missed his social worker and would have liked to have continued having contact with him. This male social worker had been important to Martin, he felt able to talk to him. He now had a female part-time social worker who had very little time to spend with Martin. Martin had learning disabilities and lived in a special residential school during the week and went to 'nan', his local authority foster carer, at the weekend. He was having some contact with his mother but none with either his stepfather or natural father, although he wanted to have contact with the latter. The social services were opposed to Martin having contact with his father because of alleged paedophile activities. Martin's father had made a contact application in the care proceedings, and was presently undergoing assessment in relation to this. Martin did not see any of his male relatives or friends. He continually asked his guardian ad litem if he could see his cousin. The guardian told Martin that he would pass this request on to his social worker. Martin spent part of his weekends at 'nan's' travelling to his old neighbourhood some miles away and attempting to see his relatives.

Martin's guardian was very aware that he was an isolated child.

'I mean [Martin] is extremely isolated. He's going to need, I suspect he is always going to need a degree of support. He is almost totally isolated from his family.'

Richard, aged 10, was living with foster carers and had also had a change of social worker during the court proceedings. He had liked his original social worker but believed that he had lost him because his parents had complained that *they* did not like him. Unfortunately they did not like the new one either.

'I've had two social workers during it [the proceedings] . . . Well my mum and dad didn't like [social worker] . . . He was okay. He's coming again tonight. Well, this is his very last time, to come and see me. I've already got [the new social worker]. Children ought to be able to choose. My mum and dad don't like the social worker I've got now . . . I don't know, if there's another one, they will almost be through all the social workers.'

Obviously the researcher did not have all the details about the change of social worker but what was important was that Richard perceived the change of his social worker as being due to his parents' dislike of the social worker rather than his own preferences. Richard felt isolated by this change. A number of guardians in the study referred to instances where they had felt that social services had reacted to the needs of the parents over those of the child or young person. Social services had to work with parents both during and after the proceedings. Some guardians felt that this parent focus detracted from the interests of the child. As one guardian stated:

'We [the solicitor and the guardian] felt that it [social services care plan for the child] was as much to do with mother's feelings that were being considered.'

Fear of isolation returning

Tom and Lee's mother had made an application for contact with them. They had had no contact with her for many years and complained that the proceedings were now upsetting their life with their foster family. Although they had been under care orders for a considerable time, they had had little contact with social services. They now had a new social worker who they felt was trying to be too involved in their lives. Their agenda was to continue the previous arrangements with no contact with their natural mother and little contact with their social worker who 'intruded' in their lives.

Originally the boys had lived with two different foster families but were later reunited in the same household. They worried that the proceedings could disrupt this stability. In effect they had a fear of becoming isolated from each other and their stable home life. The older boy had only just returned to live at the foster carers. He had left the home after clashes with them about his behaviour. He had not settled in two subsequent placements and was grateful to his foster carers for allowing him to return.

One issue resolved during the proceedings involved Lee. He wanted to go on a school trip to France but his foster carers had said that they could not afford this and that he could not go. The guardian became aware of this issue. The end result was that social services paid for Lee to go to France as he was in the local authority's care. Lee was very pleased by this development.

Martin had also witnessed other foster children having to leave his foster home because their behaviour had proved unacceptable. Unfortunately within a few weeks of this occurrence, Martin's foster carer, 'nan', announced that she was going to retire from fostering. This development concerned Martin very much. He was very anxious about where he would stay at the weekends when he was not at school. This was particularly worrying because his stepfather had barred Martin from the family home after Martin had made some disclosures about his stepfather's behaviour. Martin continually asked his school house parent, his solicitor and his guardian ad litem about this. He said he needed to know who would be his new foster carer. Each of the professionals said that they would pass on his concerns to his social worker. Weeks went by without any report back from the local authority about a new carer. On one visit the house parent informed the guardian ad litem, the solicitor and the researcher that Martin had been spending his weekends trying to find himself a new foster carer. The school had been notified that Martin had turned up at the home of some foster carers he had previously met to ask if they would consider fostering him.

Isolation – being different

Sylvia had endured considerable upheaval since the death of her mother and was still grieving. She tried to instil some normality into her life by watching her favourite television programmes, *Neighbours* and *Home And Away*. These programmes were important to Sylvia. She had been a fan for many years and talked about the story lines with her friends at school. Sylvia wanted to be able to continue to mix with her peers in this way. She explained that if she didn't watch the programmes she would be the odd one out.

Sylvia worried that she might not be allowed to watch her programmes because she had not done her homework. Her foster carer was strict: homework had to be done before the television could be switched on. Unfortunately for Sylvia, her guardian ad litem and her solicitor visited her after school, during homework time. On one visit she asked her solicitor to leave after only ten minutes so that she could do her homework and watch her programme. On another visit Sylvia got upset and asked her guardian to ask her foster carer to allow her to watch the programmes before her homework because her guardian's visit had delayed her. The guardian did this but the foster carer only replied, 'We'll see.'

Andrew, aged 15, had been doing reasonably well at school but a withdrawal of transport meant he had to change school. He had not settled and bad behaviour resulted in his exclusion. Andrew had lived with his mother and then with his grandmother but there had been arguments and Andrew had left. There was some concern that Andrew had been harshly disciplined. Andrew was placed in two separate local authority placements whilst under an interim care order. He refused to stay in each and finally moved in with an aunt who was willing to take him. Andrew wanted to remain with his aunt, under a care order to ensure that he did not have to return to live with either his mother or his grandmother. Andrew's mother opposed the application for a care order. She was unhappy about Andrew living with his aunt. Andrew had part-time tuition but was very behind in school work. His guardian confirmed that Andrew's problems developed when he changed school.

'Yes it was terrible and no one has ever been held accountable about that decision. It was an Education one . . . found it far too expensive . . . That 's what it was all about. He was doing well . . .'

Andrew asked his guardian if he thought the local authority would assist him in buying a motor bike. His guardian advised him to ask but added that they were probably more likely to consider funding for a bicycle. Andrew said that he would contact his social worker about this.

Carl has already been mentioned above because he was not happy with his social worker. Carl was already the subject of a care order. His mother had had problems related to alcohol abuse and Carl had moved to live with his aunt and cousin. His aunt's home was close to his mother's home so Carl was able to have contact with her and his two half brothers. Carl returned to live with his mother and as a result the local authority applied to discharge his care order. The same guardian and solicitor were appointed to act in the proceedings. The guardian said that she was surprised to learn that Carl had returned to live with his mother because he had been adamant that he preferred to live with his aunt. The researcher accompanied the guardian on a visit to Carl at his mother's house. Carl's mother sat by the guardian nursing her youngest child and Carl continued to play a computer type game. When the guardian asked him about his wishes, he said very little. The guardian told Carl that there would soon be a court hearing to consider the discharge of the care order.

Shortly after this visit Carl ran away from home, returning to live with his aunt. The aunt told social services that Carl did not want to live with his mother. As a result the court hearing was adjourned and the guardian arranged to see Carl at his aunt's home. The researcher went too. Carl explained that he had been pushed into going back to his mother by his social worker who he said did not listen to him. He wanted to remain at his aunt's home but to continue to have contact with his mother as before. The guardian accepted that this was Carl's choice and filed an addendum to her report recommending that Carl should remain with his aunt. Carl's solicitor did not visit him during this period although during her interview with the researcher she confirmed that he was a young man whom she would define as being competent. She stated:

'I think he probably was because he was older than his years which was one of the problems, and I think if his instructions had differed from [the guardian] I would have been able to take instructions directly from him.'

Edward, aged 10, had been brought into care as there were concerns about his care at home. Edward's mother had left his stepfather who was unwilling to care for Edward. Edward's behaviour was very disruptive at times and he had some physical disabilities that made it difficult for him to communicate verbally. Edward was not having contact with either of his parents whose whereabouts were unknown. Edward was placed with short-term foster carers who had only recently begun to foster. Edward's behaviour improved and he appeared to settle well. The foster parents' son was slightly older than Edward and they shared a bedroom together. Edward liked his company. Edward wanted to have contact with his siblings who continued to live at home with his stepfather. He also wanted to have his skateboard brought to his foster home so that he could be like the other children on the estate and join in their games.

Edward was isolated from his family and felt isolated from the other children on the estate because he did not have a skateboard. Edward told both his solicitor and his guardian that he wanted to have contact with his family and that he wanted his skateboard. The guardian promised to tell Edward's social worker about his wishes. The guardian did not see a problem in obtaining the skateboard because Edward's stepfather had agreed to the request and the local social services office was close by. Obtaining the skateboard was a priority for Edward. He had been placed with his foster carers at the end of June and was to spend the whole of the school summer holidays with them.

When the guardian visited Edward some weeks later he still did not have his skateboard. The foster carer explained that Edward and her son had had some disagreements because her son wanted to go off and play on his skateboard and Edward did not have his. Edward was increasingly isolated from playing with the other children because he did not have his skateboard. His isolation was compounded by his speech difficulties. The foster carer had offered to fetch the skateboard but had been told that social services would deal with the matter. The solicitor and guardian discussed fetching it but were unsure of the boundaries of their role. Would they be invading social services territory? Could expenses be claimed for this? They both contacted social services but were frustrated by the lack of action.

> 'We applied a lot of pressure, we did not see it as a major undertaking to get the skateboard especially as it was just a few minutes walk from the social services office. Unfortunately the social worker was pressurised by the child protection investigation and said that the skateboard was not her priority. The social worker saw the skateboard as her role and would not delegate. I couldn't see why she couldn't ask a voluntary agency to get the skateboard.'

Edward still wanted contact with his siblings. He had accidentally bumped into some of his family whilst out shopping with his foster carer. He was now continually asking if he could go and see them. Some contact was arranged and eventually Edward got his skateboard, although only towards the end of the school holidays.

At the end of the summer holidays social services decided that Edward should attend a special residential school during the week and return to his foster carers at weekends. The researcher went with the guardian to visit Edward at his new school at the beginning of the term. The head teacher explained that Edward found his move to a residential school difficult. He cried at night because he did not understand why he could not go home to his foster carers. Some pupils at the school were day pupils and were collected by minibus each evening. Edward thought that he must have done something wrong for his foster carers to send him away. He asked his guardian about this. Edward's agenda had now changed. He still wanted to have contact with his family and particularly his siblings, but he also wanted to go back to his foster carers and sleep there each night instead of being forced to stay the week at school.

MAKING AND KEEPING CONTACTS

Sylvia's extended family could not offer her a permanent home. Sylvia accepted the need for a care order but wanted to make sure that she would live nearer to her grandmother. Seeing her grandmother was important to Sylvia. During a visit with her guardian to McDonald's, Sylvia asked her guardian to take her to visit her grandmother, and reluctantly, her guardian had agreed. Sylvia also wanted to see her father who had expressed a wish to see his daughter. All the professionals agreed that Sylvia should have no contact with her father as he had been in prison following a conviction for sexually abusing her. Sylvia was adamant that she wanted to see her father and continued to ask both her guardian and her solicitor to facilitate this.

On one occasion she told her solicitor:

'I want to see my dad. He is my dad. It is my right.'

Sylvia's solicitor deflected her by telling her that the current proceedings were about her care. If Sylvia still felt that she wanted to have contact with her father then her solicitor could raise this issue on her behalf, in later proceedings, if Sylvia asked her to do so. Under the Children Act the court must consider the local authority's arrangements for contact before making a care order.

Her solicitor explained:

'I know [guardian] was saying absolutely no contact. I know the local authority wanted absolutely no contact, and I know in my own mind I wanted absolutely no contact. But I was hoping that we could get her round to seeing that at the moment it wasn't a good thing. I can understand from her point of view as to why she wanted to see her father but clearly . . . at the age she was . . . she's very vulnerable at the moment having lost her mother. And having decided that she wasn't competent . . . I mean I was happy that. Well that may be what she wanted, it wasn't the right thing for her at that age. But it's maybe something she would have to think about later on.'

Sylvia was aware that her guardian had spoken with her father and that he might attend court. Sylvia said she wanted to attend the court hearing. But shortly before the final hearing, after her solicitor had said that she could not guarantee that Sylvia's father would be attending court, Sylvia appeared to lose interest in the proceedings. Sylvia's attention then turned to getting her solicitor to talk about all her foreign holidays. Sylvia was enthralled as she had never been abroad.

Carol, aged 14, was taken into care under an interim order because there were concerns of neglect and possible abuse. Carol attended a special day school because she had learning difficulties. She was settled with her foster family, getting on well with both foster carers and their daughters. Carol's sister had been adopted and Carol had had no contact for many years. After she went into foster care, Carol was told that she could write to her sister and that her letter would be forwarded by her social worker. Carol was pleased by this development. Carol's wishes reflected an ideal. She wanted to live in a new house with her mother, father and sister. Carol said that she understood that this was not possible but was content with the knowledge that the care plan for her was to continue to live with her present foster carers and to have contact with her parents.

Edward was told that there was the possibility that he might be able to live with an aunt, who lived in another county, and that this would be a long-term placement. One of his sisters already lived with the aunt and he had some cousins there too. He was pleased with this news. Edward told his guardian that this was what he wanted.

The following week Edward's solicitor visited him, accompanied by the researcher. The solicitor wanted to hear from Edward what he wanted because the final hearing was imminent. Edward told his solicitor that he wanted to be with his mother. This information confused the solicitor. The guardian and the social worker had both reported that Edward wanted to live with his aunt. The solicitor stayed on at the school until after lunch and played football with Edward. He was able to ascertain that Edward had had a recent visit from his mother. He had not seen her for some time. In the end the solicitor deduced that Edward wished to live with his mother but if she were unable to care for him then he would be just as happy to go to live with his aunt. The solicitor explained:

'Well I stayed on because I was acutely aware that he was saying something different to [the social worker] and [the guardian]. I was aware that I had a responsibility to him and I had got to really pick up whether he really was pining for his mum and how much relevance I had got to attach to that.'

GOING TO COURT

Throughout the meetings with both her guardian and solicitor, Carol had expressed a wish to attend court. She continually referred to this. As Carol had learning difficulties, her guardian had chosen to explain the court proceedings to her from a book depicting animals. The magistrate was a wise owl, the guardian a squirrel, and the child a little rabbit. The guardian referred to the picture where all the animals meet in court but Carol was able to point out the fact that 'all' did not include a picture of the little rabbit, and the little rabbit should be present.

On another occasion Carol's solicitor explained to her that she would speak for Carol in court. Carol again stated that she wanted to attend and talked about a recent episode of the television programme *Kavanagh QC* where a man at court was able to speak to the judge in person because he did not have a solicitor. Carol thought it would be better if she could attend and speak to the judge herself. Carol's solicitor was amazed at her understanding of the television programme. Both the solicitor and the researcher had watched the episode and Carol's understanding of the court events was correct. Her solicitor explained that she did not believe that Carol, with her learning disabilities, was able to give instructions but that her understanding of some issues were quite astounding.

> 'There was that moment . . . when she related that television programme. That threw me . . . that was amazing wasn't it? I thought about that for a long time. She understands a lot more than we give her credit for. But at the end of the day I think it was a little beyond her to make decisions for herself. It was interesting in that I started off with a more closed mind about her abilities.'

Carol's guardian did not feel Carol was competent and was against her attending the final court hearing. The solicitor was guided by this but nevertheless felt that Carol's wishes should be taken on board and arranged for a directions appointment at the magistrates court so that Carol's request to attend the court hearing could be considered.

Richard was concerned to attend the final hearing at court. He had asked both his guardian and his solicitor about this. His guardian told the researcher that initially she was not in favour of this because courts were not child friendly, but that she felt that Richard was so keen to attend that she set about facilitating this. The guardian asked Richard's solicitor to ensure that someone on the bench would be able to relate to a child.

> 'So I said to the solicitor could he see what he could do about ensuring that there was somebody on the bench that knew about communicating with children.'

Richard's solicitor was on the Children Panel and represented children in care proceedings. He was also a criminal advocate and represented clients in criminal proceedings. There was the possibility that Richard might be charged with criminal activity and his solicitor was concerned that his client was not placed in any situation that could prove detrimental to any case. As such the solicitor would not agree to the researcher observing any meetings between Richard and his guardian or between Richard and his solicitor.

YOUNG PEOPLE IN SECURE ACCOMMODATION

James, Barbara, Sonia and William were all teenagers involved in applications for secure accommodation orders. By the very nature of their cases they were isolated from their family and homes. Both Barbara and William had been in secure accommodation for many months. The study applications were renewals of the secure accommodation orders.

All four young people attended their court hearings.

Barbara, a young black woman aged 15, had been fostered for many years by a white couple but was then removed and placed with black foster carers whom social services felt would address issues relating to her identity and ethnicity. Barbara's contact with her original carers was limited. The new placement broke down and her behaviour became very disturbed. She was placed in secure accommodation under the Mental Health Act because she was self-harming. She was pleased that she was now subject to a court secure accommodation order. She explained:

> 'When I came here I was put under *a section*, Mental Health Act, but they found that it wasn't going to work for me 'cause I was not mentally ill. So they took me off that and took me to court and got me a secure accommodation order. But you have to be here under something, so then they said, "Would you like to be under a secure accommodation order?" So I said, "Yes" and this place said, "Yes" . . . Because it is easier for me to get out where it is with a judge, whereas with everybody else it is with doctors.'

William, aged 15, had been placed at his current secure unit because he had indecently assaulted younger children. He had been transferred from another secure unit which had no facilities to address this behaviour. The guardian felt that this was a good move for William. Like Barbara, William was not opposing the application for renewal of the order, although he had stated that he was getting bored and might oppose the next one.

Both teenagers had got to know their respective solicitors and guardians well because they had represented them at a number of applications over many months. William's family visited him only sporadically, so he appreciated the visits from his guardian and solicitor, who sometimes brought him gifts. William was also aware that he was privileged in that his solicitor visited him at the unit. He explained:

> 'Some people in here don't see their solicitors and they only see them at court. In this unit only my solicitor comes . . . sometimes [the guardian] buys me sweets and [the solicitor] buys me fags and sometimes they swap.'

Barbara also looked forward to visits by her solicitor and guardian. Barbara had been fostered since she was a baby. Her former foster carers visited, but not as often as Barbara wanted, because they had a long way to travel. Barbara had a particularly close relationship with her solicitor. She referred to her solicitor as a friend and saw her socially, not just when an application to renew the order was made. They had been to the cinema together. Barbara had her solicitor's mobile telephone number and so was able to contact her directly.

> 'She is more like a friend. I can just phone her up whenever . . . just phone her for a chat . . . yes she makes time for me.'

James, aged 15, had got into trouble by stealing cars. Recently he had been excluded from school. James would not talk about why he had begun to act as he did. There had been some recent upheaval at home resulting in his mother's partner leaving after many years. James had never been in a secure unit and was petrified of being locked up at night and on the first night he had damaged his bedroom door. He wanted to get out of secure as quickly as possible and go home to his mother. James' mother often worked away from home and provided little supervision. James acknowledged the professionals' concern that he might get into trouble again if he was left alone during the summer holidays. He agreed with his guardian ad litem and solicitor not to oppose the application for a secure accommodation order but to work for an early release. James spent his time in the unit's gym and also attending classes on car maintenance at the unit.

James indicated to his guardian that he wanted contact with his mother's former partner. James had been brought up to believe this man was his father and had only learned that this was not the case when his mother's relationship broke down. James had no address for this man but was aware that his mother was against any contact. James' overriding agenda was to get out of the secure unit.

Sonia, aged 16, had been accommodated during some of her teens because she was beyond her mother's control. Whilst in social services care Sonia was recruited into prostitution. She was a witness in the criminal proceedings which followed. Later Sonia gave birth to a baby girl whom she cared for her at her mother's home. Out socialising one evening, Sonia got involved in a fight and as a result ended up in secure accommodation. Social services removed Sonia's child and started care proceedings. Sonia wanted contact but was told by staff from the secure unit that social services were considering adoption for the baby. As a result, she absconded from court whilst waiting to attend her secure accommodation hearing.

> 'I was frustrated. Nothing going on. No contact . . . I ran away because I wanted something sorted.'

A warrant was issued for Sonia's arrest. Her guardian ad litem left messages with Sonia's friends and family to tell her to get in touch. In response to this Sonia gave herself up. Her overriding agenda was to care for her child. She wanted to be with her. She was opposing both the application for the secure order and the care order on her child.

MISSING AGENDAS

Charles, aged 9, was one boy whose agenda remained unclear because he did not engage with the process. The proceedings were to discharge the existing care order. He was already living at home with his mother, her partner and a sibling. Charles said very little to his guardian ad litem when the researcher observed them together and his solicitor visited him only once, for a few minutes. She recalled:

'I did go to see him on my own . . . I think I saw him for about ten minutes because he was obviously more interested in playing football.'

Charles provided little information for the research but it was clear that his understanding of the process was very limited. His lack of engagement may have reflected his earlier experiences of the care proceedings. As his solicitor stated:

'But I got the feeling with [Charles] that he didn't know the significance of a care order so wasn't really bothered about it being discharged and it wasn't one of his top priorities.'

Overall, the majority of the young people in the study had agendas during the proceedings which concerned where they were going to live, who they were going to live with, and what contact they were going to have with family and friends. Professionals view court proceedings, particularly where there is representation by a guardian ad litem and a solicitor, as providing an opportunity to focus on and resolve issues for children and young people. But concerns have been expressed that too little account is taken of the impact of the process on children, young people and their families (Wells 1995). Professionals working in these proceedings might like to think that young people's agendas are directly related to the court proceedings and that the court is focusing on young people's concerns. In practice, as we will see in Chapter 8 'Children's and young people's agendas revisited', this is not necessarily the case.

4

THE SYSTEM'S AGENDA

The court system is part of a wider child welfare system which seeks to provide support for families who need assistance in bringing up their children, to protect children from significant harm, to look after children whose families are not caring for them adequately and to regulate arrangements for the care of children outside their families. Since the 1970s it has evolved in response to concerns about justice to parents, the control of local authorities, the protection of children and children's rights. Many interest groups and events have helped to determine its agenda – the issues which it focuses on and the way it approaches them.

The courts become involved with child care matters when local authorities, parents, carers or, more rarely, children refer cases to them. Courts assess evidence, determine disputes, apply legal criteria and make orders which authorise or restrict action. Local authorities seek court orders relating to the care of children where parents or carers are unwilling to accept the need for, or the extent of, involvement by the local authority social services department; also, where the local authority's actions such as placing a child in secure accommodation or restricting parental contact require sanction by the court. Parents, carers and children apply to court in order to challenge local authority decisions or to discharge the orders which gave the local authority control over the child.

Prior to the Children Act 1989, issues relating to the care of children by local authorities could be dealt with in magistrates' courts, county courts or the High Court, each operating under a separate legal code with differing standards, powers and procedures (Maidment 1981). The majority of cases were dealt with at the lowest level of court, by lay magistrates, applying the Children and Young Persons Act 1969. However, during the 1980s local authorities made increasing use of the High Court's inherent jurisdiction, applying for orders to make children wards of court and to commit them to care (Masson and Morton 1989). These cases were heard by High Court judges but not necessarily by specialists in child care law. The Children Act 1989 ended this use of the High Court's inherent jurisdiction and replaced the various powers to commit children to care with a single statutory code. All three levels of civil court, the magistrates' court renamed the family proceedings court, the county court and the High Court, were given equivalent powers and procedures in care proceedings. All magistrates and judges hearing these cases had special training (CAAC 1992, 10). Provision was made for the transfer of cases between courts to ensure that they were heard at a level appropriate to their complexity.

INDEPENDENT SCRUTINY OF APPLICATIONS

The expectation that there will be an independent scrutiny of the application is implicit in the reference of any matter to a court. The focus of this scrutiny and its nature depend on the criteria set out in legislation, including the scope for judicial discretion and the court's powers of disposal. The procedures available to the court, the status of the court and court culture determine its extent.

Court scrutiny of applications in care proceedings under the Children and Young Persons Act 1969 was initially very limited despite a requirement to have regard to the child's welfare (CYPA 1933, s. 44), discretion to make orders 'as it thinks fit' and the power to discharge them if this was 'appropriate' (CYPA 1969, ss. 1(2), 21(2)). The court could only choose from a very limited range of orders. Moreover, the procedures severely limited the information available to the court for making its decisions. The court had no independent source of information but, as in other civil or criminal proceedings, was dependent on the parties. The information provided by the parties was partial and limited, leaving the court with an incomplete picture of the child's circumstances. Although it was accepted that 'the real issue is nearly always between the local authority and the parent' (*R. v. Worthing Justices ex p. Stevenson* 1976, Widgery C.J.) the parties to the proceedings were the local authority and the child. Parents had only the most limited rights to participate and no entitlement to legal aid. Before 1980 parents generally instructed the child's legal representative (Law Society 1979); subsequently, until the introduction of the guardian ad litem system, solicitors for children frequently had to work without instructions (Dingwall and Eekelaar 1983, 173–174). The parties were also hampered in their ability to focus the court on the issues by the lack of disclosure of evidence before the hearing and the fact that they had no rights of access to information held by the local authority. The results of inadequate scrutiny could be devastating:

'In November 1971, a mother applied for the discharge of a care order in respect of her daughter, Maria Colwell, a 6 year old girl who had been living with foster carers since she was a few months old. The application was not opposed by the local authority and the court was given no information which suggested that it should be refused. The foster carers were not notified of the proceedings and had no rights to participate in them. The court revoked the order, substituting a supervision order. A year later Maria died having

suffered repeated, physical abuse from her step-father. The Committee of Inquiry established to investigate the circumstances identified numerous failures
by those involved and suggested that the court would have been helped by an
independent social work report against which it could test the report of the
local authority social worker.' (DHSS 1974, para. 227)

Procedural change to improve the court's access to information and facilitate scrutiny of applications was slow. Provision was made in the Children
Act 1975, s. 64 for the court to order that the parents were not to be treated as
representing the child and to appoint a guardian ad litem for the child, but,
until 1984, partial implementation limited this to unopposed applications for
discharge of care and supervision orders. The court retained a discretion not
to appoint a guardian ad litem and practices varied. Scrutiny by the court
was also linked to justice to parents; where the court ordered that parents
could not represent the child it could also order that they should have legal
aid 'for the purpose of taking such part in the proceedings as may be allowed by the rules of court' (Legal Aid Act 1974, s. 28(6A)). Parents only
obtained full rights to participate 'as parties' with legal aid in 1988 when the
Children and Young Persons (Amendment) Act 1986 was implemented.

The court's status and culture did not encourage challenge of the local
authority's case. The magistrates had little training, and sitting part-time
they could gather only limited experience of care cases. Empirical evidence
indicated that applications by local authorities were usually successful (Hilgendorf 1981, 102; Dingwall and Eekelaar 1983, 206). Although, in 1984,
magistrates were given jurisdiction to review local authority decisions about
contact to children in care, applying the welfare principle, they were expected to exercise this in ways which supported the local authority's plans
(*Re L.H.* 1986, Sheldon J.).

Introduction of the guardian ad litem system gave the court an independent,
social work trained, child care expert with an obligation to investigate all the
relevant circumstances, interview persons, inspect records and write a report
for the court (Magistrates' Courts (Children and Young Persons) (Amendment)
Rules 1984, r. 14A). The involvement of guardians ad litem did influence proceedings, particularly through the work they did before the hearing (Masson
and Shaw 1988, 176). However, court scrutiny of applications was largely restricted to testing the evidence because of the limited powers of the magistrates
and the practice of endorsing local authority applications.

Welfare

The court's scrutiny is not only focused on assessing whether the local
authority has produced evidence which establishes that the conditions for
orders are met. Except in cases concerning secure accommodation orders (*Re*

M. 1996), the court's paramount consideration is now the welfare of the child (Children Act 1989, s. 1(1)). In contested cases and applications for care, supervision and contact orders the court is guided in its application of the welfare principle by a checklist of factors (s. 1(3)). In all cases the court must also establish that the 'no order principle' is satisfied, i.e. that it is better for the child to make the proposed order than to make no order at all (s. 1(5)).

The duties of the guardian ad litem and the child's solicitor both reflect the emphasis on welfare. The guardian ad litem is required to have regard to the welfare checklist when carrying out his or her duties and to file a report advising on the interests of the child (FPR r. 4.11(1), (7)). The solicitor for the child is required to take instructions from the guardian unless the child is competent to give instructions and is in conflict with the guardian. Where there is no guardian and no instructions from the child, the solicitor must conduct the case to further the child's best interests (r. 4.12(1)). The child's wishes are relevant; the child's wishes and feelings are an aspect of welfare included in the checklist. The guardian must advise the court about the child's wishes.

The emphasis on welfare has to be tempered by an acceptance that the court must operate justly and has to apply the current law. In practice, the court can only select what is in the child's best interests from the options available. The implementation of the order in ways which further the child's welfare is the responsibility of the parents, local authority and those caring for the child.

DIVISION OF RESPONSIBILITY BETWEEN COURTS AND LOCAL AUTHORITIES

Before the Children Act 1989

Not all matters relating to the treatment of individual children by the child welfare system were under the control of the courts. The magistrates' courts could decide whether to make an order but they had no power over how the child was cared for subsequently. The High Court, exercising its inherent jurisdiction, could commit a child into the care of the local authority and issue detailed directions about how the child, its ward, should be looked after. Thus issues, such as the child's placement and the arrangements for contact, which were dealt with by local authorities after care proceedings had ended, were dealt with by the High Court in wardship. In theory, all major decisions relating to wards had to be referred back to the court. In practice, judicial power was more limited. The court had no system for monitoring what was happening to its wards unless matters were brought before it; in some cases, local authorities treated wards like other children in care without any reference to their special legal status (Masson and Morton,

1989). The High Court's greater power over local authority decisions did not apparently discourage local authorities from using it. There were advantages in referring contentious matters to this court; decisions were made on the basis of the child's welfare without any restrictive criteria, evidence rules were less stringent and procedures were more flexible (Hunt 1993).

In *A. v. Liverpool C.C.* 1982 the House of Lords held that the High Court's powers in wardship could not be used to challenge local authority action. General court supervision of local authority action was only available by Judicial Review proceedings which could only be used if a local authority had acted illegally, irrationally or contrary to natural justice. Judicial Review only enables the court to strike down decisions, not to determine the way in which a local authority should provide for children in its care. This was both a constitutional and a practical issue. Social services departments could not function within the framework created by statute if the courts had power to review every decision; courts lacked the means and experience to make decisions in relation to the myriad of matters which arise in the care of children.

The need to clarify and separate the roles of courts and local authorities was recognised by the Social Services Select Committee on Children in Care and the Review of Child Care Law. 'The expertise of a court lies in its ability to hear all sides of the case, to determine issues of fact and to make a firm decision on a particular issue at a particular time, in accordance with the applicable law' (DHSS 1985, para. 2.23–4). The Review acknowledged that there could be different views about which decisions were appropriate for courts but considered that courts could not realistically be given the function of reviewing the case of every child in care. Nor could all disputes be dealt with by the courts, which could be inaccessible and intimidating; speedier and more informal mechanisms were required.

Court control and local authority independence under the Children Act 1989

The Children Act 1989 aimed to 'strike a balance between the rights of children to express their views on decisions made about their lives, the rights of parents to exercise their responsibilities towards the child and the duty of the state to intervene where the child's welfare requires it' (DH 1991, para. 1.1). To this end the Act established a specialist court system and clarified and streamlined the powers of the court in care proceedings. Both parents and children had party status and access to legal aid. The duty to appoint a guardian was strengthened and applied to a wider range of proceedings. Guardians were given responsibility to advise the court on aspects of case management such as timetabling. Together these reforms facilitated the proper scrutiny of applications.

It is clear that the Children Act 1989 both increased the obligation on the courts to determine whether and what orders should be made in care proceedings and removed the power of the High Court to supervise local authority action through the inherent jurisdiction. Courts lost the power to commit children to care without an application by a local authority but gained powers to review decisions about contact with children in care to the extent of being able to state when, where and how often contact should take place and to make contact orders in care proceedings even though no application had been made.

Official guidance states that 'the courts have an independent duty to do what is best for the child. If the courts are to discharge that duty they will often have to take an active part in the proceedings rather than simply act as umpires between the contending parties' (DH 1990, para. 1.51). However, courts can only refuse orders or select from a (wider) menu of orders, they cannot make a full care or supervision order unless a local authority brings care proceedings nor can they impose conditions when making care orders (*Re T.* 1994, Wall J.; *Re. P.* 1993, Waite L.J.). Care orders are final orders and only subject to any court review if an application is made for their discharge.

The balance between court control and local authority independence under the Children Act is a matter of some controversy (Dewar 1995, 25; Thorpe and Clarke 1998). The extent of the court's power to control and review local authority decision-making relating to child care is unclear and different views have been expressed about whether the courts should have greater powers over local authorities (Dewar 1995; Hayes 1996; BAAF 1997; Hunt and Macleod 1997). The local authority's plan for the child's care when the final order in care proceedings is made has become the locus for the court's exercise of power over the local authority. Once the threshold criteria for an order have been satisfied, a consideration of the care plan and of any alternative proposals for the child's care enables the court to determine what, if any, order is in the child's best interests and also to ensure that the welfare of the child is its paramount consideration. In exercising this power courts have to be aware that the local authority controls its own resources and cannot be made to implement the care plan in any particular way. Nor can the court legitimately retain control by continually making interim orders where no matters are outstanding (*Re J.* 1994, Wall J.; *Re P.* 1993, Waite L.J.).

The court rules require the local authority to disclose its care plan in care proceedings and, according to Wall J. this should be subject to 'rigorous scrutiny' but

> '[I]n each case the evidence which requires to be called to satisfy the court as to the efficacy of the care plan will vary in substance and degree, it is a matter for the good sense of the tribunal and the advocates appearing before it to see that a proper balance is struck between the need to satisfy the court about the appropriateness of the care plan on the one hand and the avoidance, on the

other, of over-zealous investigation into matters which are properly within the administrative discretion of the local authority.' (*Re J.* 1994, Wall J.)

Where the court is dissatisfied with the care plan it can refuse to make the order sought but only where this course would be in the best interests of the child. Where there is no alternative plan and the child needs protection, the court is forced to accept the local authority's plan.

The guardian ad litem is required, by rules of court, to carry out the investigations which are necessary to advise the court about various matters specified in the rules, particularly its options and any other matter on which the court seeks advice (FPR r. 4.11(4),(9)). The guardian ad litem has the right to inspect all the local authority's records relating to the child or young person, including material which might otherwise be regarded as confidential, such as assessments of prospective adoptive parents or foster carers (Children Act 1989, s. 42), and it has been considered right for the guardian to do so where this information impinged on the court's decision about the order to make (*Re T.* 1994). The relevance of information may only become clear at the end of an investigation; matters which needed to be investigated may not be appropriate for court discussion if the boundary between the court's role and that of the local authority is to be maintained.

The approach to contact issues has been somewhat different. The courts acknowledged the major changes in the Children Act 1989 by accepting that their exercise of power over contact could involve some review of the care plan.

> 'Contact must not be allowed to destabilise or endanger the long term arrangements for the child and in many cases the plans for the child will be decisive of the contact application. The proposals of the local authority based on its appreciation of the best interests of the child, must command the greatest respect, but Parliament has given to the court, and not to the local authority, the duty to decide on contact. Consequently the court may have the task of requiring the local authority to justify their long-term plans to the extent only that those plans exclude contact between parent and child.' (*Re B.* 1993, Butler-Sloss L.J.).

Overall this suggests a greater willingness on the part of the courts to evaluate the arrangements for contact in the care plan. The courts have accepted that issues of contact are secondary to those of ensuring that the child has a home and is properly looked after but have asserted their power over relationships between parents and children through the making of contact and adoption orders (*Berkshire C.C. v. B.* 1997). But where there is a care order, including an interim order, the local authority decides on the child's placement. The location of the child's home and the quality of care provided are completely beyond the control of the court.

In contrast, some courts have been willing to cede their power by making orders for contact 'at the local authority's discretion'. Where such an order is made a parent can only apply to have it varied if he or she can show that there has been a change in circumstances (*Re T.* 1997). The court's power is further limited by the power of the local authority to vary court orders by agreement with the person concerned, and with the child if he or she has sufficient understanding (Contact with Children Regulations 1991, reg. 3). Each year approximately two thousand orders relating to contact are made, only 60% of these related to the granting of contact (Judicial Statistics 1996, table 5.2). If no order is made the local authority remains under a duty to allow contact; consequently the court may decide that no order is required (Children Act 1989, ss. 1(5), 34(1)).

AVOIDING CONFLICT

Judicial statements in the 1970s emphasised that, in care proceedings, the court was not an adversarial forum but had an inquisitorial role (*Humberside C.C. v. D.P.R.* 1977, Widgery C.J.). Although proceedings could be contested, the absence of full rights to participate and legal representation limited a parent's ability to challenge the local authority. Conflict was avoided by default but developed as opportunities arose for parents, carers and children to contest the local authority's case. When the Children Act was first implemented the President of the Family Division expressed the hope that it would end the adversarial approach to care cases (*B. v. Derbyshire C.C.* 1992).

The Children Act sought to provide a basis for cooperative relations between local authorities and all involved in the care of children. The emphasis on partnership with parents is strongest when services are provided by agreement and without recourse to court orders but the existence of court orders does not detract from the local authority's duties to continue to involve parents (DH 1992, para. 2.21). That being the case, it is important that the conduct of the proceedings should, as far as possible, not exacerbate the conflict. It has been suggested that the court should view the local authority as a partner (*Hounslow L.B.C. v. A.* 1993), not to collude but because the Children Act 1989 cannot work in the full interests of children unless there is a trusting relationship between local authorities and courts (Waller 1997, 192).

Although the Children Act is a complex piece of legislation, the President of the Family Division has rejected the idea that litigation should involve a strict legalistic analysis of its statutory meaning rather than its spirit (*Newham L.B.C. v. A.G.* 1993, Brown P.). Proceedings are not adversarial (*Oxfordshire C.C. v. M.* 1994, Brown P.). Where there is agreement about the grounds for a care order it is inappropriate for the court to carry out a detailed investigation of the facts (*Devon C.C. v. S.* 1992; *Re G.* 1994). Disputes over expert evidence can confuse and prolong proceedings and, for this reason, experts should meet and identify areas of agreement before the final hearing (*Re C.* 1995; *Manchester City Council v. B.* 1996).

The avoidance of conflict in the court may move disputes elsewhere. Concerns have been expressed in relation to the way the guardian ad litem service complaints procedure has been used against guardians. A Department of Health working party acknowledged the need for effective complaints mechanisms for the public but considered that there was a need for a change in culture with more emphasis on discussion, mediation and resolution (DH and WO 1996, para. 5.22). It concluded that 'other professionals must be dissuaded from using complaints for intimidatory purposes' (para. 10.1).

Although the jurisdiction of the High Court in Judicial Review remains, the requirement for local authorities to establish internal complaints systems provides a simpler method for seeking redress. The rule that other remedies must be exhausted before seeking Judicial Review means that the complaints process is also a restraint on court action (*R. v. Kingston upon Thames R.B.C. ex p. T.* 1994). The courts also view the internal complaints process as a more appropriate mechanism for dealing with disputes about the provision of services to children in need (*R. v. Birmingham C.C. ex p. A.* 1997).

MINIMISING DELAY

Delay has long been seen as a problem in cases concerning children (Goldstein, Freud and Solnit 1973, 40). The child's sense of time is different from that of adults; even a few weeks waiting may seem a very long time. Delay is stressful and stress may undermine carers' ability to look after a child. Emphasis in welfare-based decisions on maintaining the status quo may mean that delay closes options for the court. Research on care proceedings and wardship indicated that delay had become both accepted and endemic (Masson and Morton 1989, 780). The Review of Child Care Law considered a number of changes to speed up care proceedings, particularly the introduction of greater restrictions on renewing interim orders and even the introduction of maximum periods (DHSS 1985, 17.16, 17.25).

The Children Act sought to challenge the 'culture of acceptable delay' (Murch 1987, para. 2.3.6) by stating as a general principle that 'delay is likely to prejudice the welfare of the child', by requiring the court to set a timetable for the proceedings (Children Act 1989, ss. 1(2) and 32) and by giving guardians ad litem additional responsibilities related to the management of proceedings (DH 1995, 70). Only planned and purposeful delay which may be potentially beneficial to the child is acceptable (*C. v. Solihull M.B.C.* 1993, Ward J.). 'The importance of reducing the cost and delay of civil litigation makes it necessary for the court to assert greater control over the preparation for and conduct of proceedings than hitherto has been customary' (*President's Practice Note* 1995). Failure to conduct cases economically can be penalised by orders for costs (*Practice Direction* 1994). There are some indications that the courts are prepared to take a robust view on applications within proceedings which will lead to delay (*H. v. Cambridgeshire C.C.* 1996; *London Borough of Croydon v. R.* 1997).

The Children Act Advisory Committee maintained pressure on all involved to eliminate delay by monitoring the duration of proceedings and publishing the results. The Lord Chancellor's Department also commissioned a special study by Booth J. into the causes of delay (Booth 1996, para. 2.1.2). Local committees of those working in and with the courts in family cases, Family Court Business Committees, have been encouraged to address local causes of delay. Resources, particularly the availability of judicial time, remain a major problem and increase the pressure on all involved in proceedings to be prepared so hearings can be completed rather than adjourned. Nevertheless, the problem of delay appears to be particularly intractable; the average length of proceedings has increased year on year since the introduction of the Children Act.

CONCLUSION

Although the child's welfare is the court's paramount consideration in most proceedings under the Children Act 1989, the court cannot simply be viewed as a welfare agency. The court has its own agenda: to do justice by scrutinising applications in order to establish both whether the statutory criteria for orders can be met on the available evidence and whether an order is in the child's interests; to manage its business speedily and effectively; and to maintain the boundaries of its role. Different aspects of this agenda conflict; for example, detailed scrutiny may preclude speed, and speed may undermine justice. The court has only limited powers (and resources); these determine what can be on its agenda and the ways agenda items can be taken forward. Ultimately in care proceedings, including discharge and residence applications, the court's power is to determine who has parental responsibility for the child; in secure accommodation cases the court order permits or forbids the young person's detention.

5

BECOMING A REPRESENTATIVE FOR CHILDREN AND YOUNG PEOPLE

The research is only a window upon the practices of guardians and solicitors as representatives for the children and young people. It focuses upon the young people's understanding of this representation. The researcher attended almost all the visits that the guardians made to the children, after the first visit. On two occasions, decisions were taken for the representative to visit the child on their own. One guardian wanted to discuss allegations of sexual abuse and said that this discussion would be more productive with only the guardian present. The researcher was unable to observe three visits because they clashed with observation on other cases.

The researcher attended almost all the visits made by the solicitors although there were four cases where the researcher was asked not to attend the first visit as the guardian was introducing the solicitor to the child. One solicitor, who practised in both civil and criminal law, objected to the researcher observing his meetings with the child and the guardian's meetings with the child. This solicitor was also advising the child in relation to criminal charges. The solicitor was concerned to protect his client should he make any disclosures of criminal activity in front of the researcher. There were two solicitors who did not visit the young person at all and another two who only saw the children once, just for a few minutes.

THE APPOINTMENT OF THE GUARDIAN AD LITEM

The Court Rules provide that the court should appoint a guardian ad litem as soon as practicable after the commencement of the specified proceedings unless this is not necessary to safeguard the interests of the child (FPR r. 4(10)(1)). Panel administrators must therefore identify available guardians without delay. Guardians will often be appointed within 24 hours of a request. Both of the panels studied routinely appointed guardians on the day the request was made.

The guardians ad litem in the study were all selected for appointment to their cases by panel staff. Appointments were made according to the guardian's workload and availability but if someone on the panel had previously acted as a child's guardian they were reappointed where possible; this occurred for four children in the study. Panel staff contacted guardians, usually by telephone, to ascertain if the guardian could take a case. Guardians were given very brief details at this point. Subsequently, applications and supporting statements would be faxed or collected.

Ethnicity

There is no requirement in the Children Act or regulations for panels of guardians ad litem to reflect the ethnic composition of the area in which they operate although local authorities are required 'to have regard to the different racial groups to which children within their area' belong when arranging for the provision of day care or recruiting foster carers (Children Act 1989, sched. 2). Court Rules require guardians to apply the welfare principle including the welfare checklist (FPR r. 4.11(1)); they must therefore consider each child's background. The relevance of the child's gender, race, culture, religion and language and disability is affirmed in Standard 7 of the National Standards (DH and WO 1995, 16).

Six guardians in the study thought it would be useful to know the child's ethnic background at the time of appointment. This could have a bearing on the selection of the guardian and the guardian's choice of solicitor to be appointed to represent the child. This would also allow the guardian to comply with obligations under the rules and the National Standards. Local authorities and other applicants should already have this information but there is no provision for its inclusion on the application forms for the court. This is so even though the court forms were recently revised; the latest version was introduced in January 1995.

One guardian recalled that she had had to employ a black consultant on one case, because both she and the solicitor for the child were Caucasian and the young person was of mixed race. The guardian had not been aware of the child's ethnicity at the time of her appointment or at the time she appointed the solicitor for the child.

Another guardian stated:

> 'I do not know the ethnic background of the child at the time of the appointment. The form has no details for this. The guardian may not always know the reason for the application such as the relevance to sexual abuse or learning disabilities.'

Yet another guardian referred to a reluctance by the courts to highlight ethnicity:

'There is a strong resistance by the court to identify the ethnicity of the child.'

A further guardian also referred to the lack of information on ethnic background:

'It is a matter of contention about how much information is available to the guardian when appointed. There are no details on the application form about the details of origin of the child. Sometimes you can guess from the form, or the panel manager is able to recognise the family name from other proceedings, but it should not be guesswork. Details of origin are significant. It has been an issue but there is no change in the application form as yet. It wouldn't take a lot and it would raise awareness. A black solicitor or consultant may be necessary, particularly if the guardian is white. I have raised this issue with the panel manager but it would appear that the powers that be do not want the issue highlighted on the form.'

The guardian had been so concerned about this issue in relation to one past case that she asked the solicitor for the child to write to the appropriate director of social services requesting that this information be added to the court forms in the future. Social services agreed to do this. The solicitor also wrote to the Children Act Advisory Committee (CAAC) in an effort to obtain agreement nationally. The committee considered the request but decided that this information should not be included. No reasons were given.

The reasons for this reluctance were unclear. Suggestions included the fact that highlighting the ethnicity of the child was open to 'racist' criticism.

There are many children from minority ethnic or mixed backgrounds involved in public law proceedings (Barn 1993; Hunt and Macleod 1997). The Department of Health has required guardian panels to supply details of the ethnicity of children involved in specified proceedings since 1993 (DH 1995c). Panels are aware of the need to have guardians whose origins include those from minority ethnic backgrounds.

As the Department of Health Overview of Guardian Panel Annual Reports for 1992 states:

'Panels were also concerned to ensure that there was a sufficient number of guardians in membership and to increase the proportion of guardians from black and other ethnic backgrounds.' (DH 1992b, 30)

Many panels have had special advertising campaigns. There have been difficulties recruiting black and Asian guardians. The largest of all the panels, the Inner and North London Panel, recruited eight new black and Asian panel members between April 1995 and March 1996 following special advertising and continues to recruit. Its annual report of 1995/6 makes reference to this issue:

> 'The proportion of our panel members who are from minority ethnic backgrounds has increased during the year to 18 per cent. However, this still does not equate with the numbers of children served by the panel who are from different ethnic backgrounds. We shall continue to use positive action and, once it has been agreed, the Panel's Equal Opportunities Policy, to seek to correct this imbalance.'

The two panels under study reflected the general shortage of guardians from minority ethnic backgrounds. In practice it may not have been possible, in the cases studied, to have matched the ethnic background of the young people with a guardian from an appropriate background. However, without information about the child's ethnicity it was impossible for the panel administrator even to consider appointing guardians from any of the minority ethnic communities, or perhaps to consider white guardians with experience of working with those from minority ethnic backgrounds. At least with the child's ethnic details to hand, the appointed guardian would still be able to consider appointing a solicitor with such particular skills, although this would depend on the guardian's own knowledge, as the Law Society's Children Panel list of solicitors does not give this information. Languages spoken by or offered by solicitors (i.e. spoken by somone within the firm) are listed.

In the wider study sample, however, two black young people both had white guardians and white solicitors, as did all the children in the interview sample. One guardian confirmed that she had been able to appoint an Asian female solicitor for an Asian female child because she was aware of the child's ethnicity at the time of appointment. The solicitor did not speak the same language as that used by the child to communicate with her non-English-speaking parents but the solicitor's firm did offer this language. The guardian stated that her overriding concern had been to appoint an appropriate solicitor because the case involved allegations of sexual abuse. An Asian barrister was also instructed when the case was transferred to the county court. The guardian saw such appointments as crucial to the best interests of the child.

Continuity of appointment

All the guardians appointed remained the appointed representatives for the young people throughout the proceedings, although one male guardian could recall a past case where he stood down as guardian for a female child, in favour of a female guardian, because the case concerned issues of sexual abuse by a male relative.

Children and young people involved in public law proceedings have a lot of upheavals and meet a great number of professionals appointed to look into different aspects of their case. Whilst a number of children mentioned that they would like to change their social worker, none said that they wanted to change their guardian.

One reason for this was highlighted by Richard, who had already had a change of social worker although this was not by his choice:

> '[I would have] stuck with her [guardian] . . . it's better than having it all changed again, ain't it? . . . Especially when you've already had most people invited into your life.'

Extra changes may only lead to more intrusion into children's lives. Richard had already been told by his guardian that her involvement was only short term. Indeed all the guardians in the study confirmed that they would explain their short-term role to children early on, often at the first visit.

Half the children in the study sample had previously been involved in court proceedings with a guardian ad litem; five children were being represented by a guardian or a solicitor who had represented them in earlier proceedings, either an application for a care order which was now being discharged or a previous application for a secure accommodation order. For all the other children both the solicitor and guardian were new.

For some young people, keeping the same solicitor and guardian appeared to be beneficial. They established a good relationship with the professionals, even contacting their solicitor directly, and were clear that their wishes were known and being represented. For others, it could be disadvantageous. Solicitors and guardians made fewer visits, although it was not clear whether this was because they felt they knew enough about the child or young person's circumstances or because the proceedings were uncontentious. Whatever the reason, this approach gave the impression that the young person did not need to be involved and meant that their current wishes might not be adequately represented.

THE GUARDIAN ROLE

Guardians are appointed by the court; their duties include appointing a solicitor for the child and advising the court about the child's wishes and feelings. A major element of their role is to provide a report for the court advising on the interests of the child. All the guardians in the study had a background in social work, with a wealth of experience in child development. Many of them had long experience in this role; eight of the 15 guardians interviewed confirmed that they first acted in this role when the system was established in 1984. Guardians were aware that the court relied upon and appreciated the expertise of the guardian, particularly the magistrates.

> 'This is quite a big thing . . . we have had a big debate about this . . . I feel I ought to apologise to people like the social worker, because quite often . . . at the end of the hearing the magistrate goes, "Thank you very much for a very thorough report Mrs [name]" and that's it and you curl up . . . Because you think the social worker has done 20 times more than I have in terms of the amount of work with the family. And they don't get a mention. And you think, you know, all I have done is come in . . . okay . . . you have the responsibility of doing your work and making recommendations but haven't had the responsibility of doing all the nitty gritty work. And you are the one getting the praise. That quite often happens.'

> 'I'm not saying my point of view is necessarily the right one, but I think it has got a bit more chance of being right than magistrates' viewpoint . . .'

Guardians did, however, acknowledge that they lacked the legal expertise required and so relied upon the solicitor for this.

> '. . . leave the law to the lawyers and I think that is quite interesting, this thing, leaving the law to the lawyers and I do respect solicitors and their advice and their . . . the advice that they give me. And I do . . . I think I distinguish more and more between my role and theirs now.'

The appointment of the solicitor

In contrast with the practice before the Children Act 1989, it was the norm in the study areas for the guardian to appoint the solicitor for the child. Guardians were keen they should appoint the solicitor for the child and saw this as an important part of their role. Occasionally the court appointed solicitors if there was a delay in appointing a guardian. This was acceptable to the guardians because the courts appointed specialist solicitors from the Children Panel. The guardians appointed all but two of the solicitors in the study cases. One solicitor had been appointed to represent the young person in criminal proceedings, the other had been appointed by the court to represent the child in an ex parte application for an emergency protection order before a guardian had been appointed.

A number of guardians in the study referred to the fact that they often appointed solicitors for children within a short time of their own appointments. There may be court hearings that were imminent, necessitating a solicitor to act for the child. Any delays in such appointments could adversely affect the case in relation to safeguarding the best interests of the child.

This meant that when selecting the solicitor, the guardian could only take account of information he or she acquired initially.

The guardians all had a small number of solicitors whom they preferred to instruct because they had confidence in their ability and could work with them.

> 'I am happy with the system that I appoint solicitors. I have a handful of solicitors that I like. They have to be solicitors that I get on with. In the majority of cases they will, after all, be taking their instructions from me. Obviously the guardian and solicitor have to get on as well as being gender appropriate to the case.'

> 'I won't appoint a solicitor that I haven't seen in court.'

> 'I like to go with an experienced solicitor and we work extremely closely solicitors and guardians . . . if I am really busy and I've got a problem, I have to feel confident that that solicitor will actually cover the work for me and some-times that does mean the solicitor going and informing the child of certain things.'

Guardians usually decided which solicitor to appoint before they met the child but one young person had been involved in the decision and she was very positive about this involvement and had developed a strong relation-ship with her solicitor.

> 'Someone got a list of solicitors and we chose her. I went and met her . . . I just liked her attitude . . . she was really good and she actually listened to what you say. She is more than a friend . . .'

Guardians were clear that they expected solicitors to work in a particular way and would only instruct those who agreed. For example, most guard-ians expected the solicitor to see the child but one also said that she would not instruct a solicitor who would visit the child without her being there.

> 'In the bad old days, which I regard them as, when we were told which solicitor we were having, there was one or two who I used to absolutely loathe having because you'd have to twist their arm to go and see the children. That's because they had no rapport with children. I always made them go.'

Solicitors responded to guardians' preferences by varying the way they handled cases to fit with the guardian's expectations.

> 'I find I am more proactive with some guardians than with others. Some guardians just expect me to turn up at court and will probably make an ap-pointment to see me and brief me with what is going on . . . With other guardians I tend to go around with them seeing everybody involved in the case. I am quite happy to do it regardless.'

There has been some debate about whether guardians should be able to select the child's solicitor. Most solicitors accepted that they would have to get to know guardians in order to be appointed; this was one reason they participated in meetings and joint training events with guardians. They understood that giving choice to guardians helped to ensure that able solicitors were appointed for children.

Some solicitors, particularly those newly appointed to the Children Panel, had complained to the Law Society that they were not getting the appointments they felt they deserved. The Law Society and some individual solicitors have suggested that a rota system should be reintroduced so that all members of the Children Panel gain experience. None of the guardians favoured such a system. One GALRO panel manager had received complaints from solicitors about their lack of appointments:

> 'I have been written to by some solicitors saying that they are not getting . . . part of our review procedure . . . is to ensure that a range of solicitors are being used . . . but that is as far as I would take it to ensure that panel members are not getting tied up with one particular solicitor. When new people come onto the panel, I circulate availability but after that it is really up to them. We are quite fortunate here . . . we have quite a small group of solicitors. The child care panel isn't huge. It is quite a tight group and with the . . . number of guardians they do get to know each other fairly well . . .'

As discussed above, it was difficult for guardians to take account of the child's ethnicity when appointing solicitors as this information was not at hand. Generally, however, guardians did know the age and gender of the child when appointing solicitors and this information was taken into consideration when choosing a solicitor for the child.

One solicitor stated:

> 'It is important that the solicitor is chosen with the case and the child in mind. I am totally opposed to any sort of rota based system. For example, I have experience of cases involving teenage girls . . .'

One male guardian explained his practice:

> '. . . Certainly if I was representing a girl, then I would appoint a female solicitor . . .'

Only one girl was represented by two men, although her original guardian had been a woman. Four boys were represented only by women; in all but one instance these children had siblings of the opposite sex who were involved in the proceedings. In eight cases, male guardians had appointed female solicitors, or female guardians had appointed male solicitors; in six cases both guardian and solicitor were female, and in three, male.

'I try and spread the work around. I never go back to the same one at all. Which I know occasionally guardians do and I think that's very wrong. I mean I think there's pros and cons . . . if you work well with somebody. But I think there's also danger of being very cosy as well with solicitors. So first of all . . . what's the reason for the proceedings and obviously if it's sexual abuse of a child, particularly a female, I would always look towards a woman solicitor. Not necessarily always. But that would be one of my factors . . . I had a run of girls who had been sexually abused so I was appointing women solicitors but not always the same woman.'

'I felt I needed to have somebody who would think through carefully the implications of [the child's] offences. And I didn't particularly want a female, given the nature of the charges.'

Guardians referred to secure accommodation applications where conflict could arise between the young person and the guardian about the appointment of solicitors. Young people involved in criminal proceedings would usually have appointed their criminal solicitor prior to the involvement of a guardian. Some young people may have had the same criminal solicitor for some years and others had instructed a solicitor who had met them through the police station rota. Some had been pleased that their solicitor 'plea bargained' on their behalf and wanted to retain them. Guardians, on the other hand, wanted to appoint a solicitor of their choice from the Children Panel. Sometimes the young people opposed this and sometimes the opposition came from the existing solicitors.

This became an issue for one guardian in a study case; eventually the young person consented to a new solicitor from the Children Panel. The guardian stated:

'And in the case of secure accommodation applications . . . I always feel that it is helpful to know whether the child has already got a solicitor. 'Cause often the difficulty about that in secure applications, particularly in relation to boys . . . A secure order for a boy may involve a certain level of criminal activity, in which case they will have had representation . . . legal representation. Often they want to continue with that solicitor or that solicitor, unfortunately, wants to continue with them. But then you find that solicitor, who has represented them, maybe for years, for the criminal stuff . . . is not on the Children Panel. And he's new to the ball game of secure accommodation and welfare grounds . . . and that's really important because the tendency is to get their client to admit things or not admit things . . . because those are the rules of the criminal court. And it's totally different in the welfare capacity and what the Children Act is about . . . because they see a good solicitor as somebody who's got them off . . . or plea bargained for them.'

Three of the four solicitors involved in the four secure accomodation applications were appointed by the guardians and were members of the Children Panel. The fourth solicitor, also a member of the Children Panel, had been appointed by the young person prior to the involvement of the guardian. All the solicitors appointed to act for the children in the study remained the legal representatives for the children throughout the case.

One solicitor recalled an earlier case where a young man, aged 13 years, had walked into her office and asked her to represent him in his public law proceedings because he was not happy with his present representatives. Although the young man had both a solicitor and a guardian, the new solicitor was given leave by the court to represent him. The existing solicitor stayed with the guardian. The solicitor saw the case as unique. She had not anticipated that the court would grant her leave to act and did not foresee a reoccurrence.

THE SOLICITOR ROLE

All the solicitors representing children in the interview study cases were members of the Law Society Children Panel. They saw themselves as specialists in this area of work, combining it with a general family practice or criminal work. This was also the case for all but two of the solicitors who represented children in the wider sample where the researchers had no access to the young person. Of these two, one had applied to join the panel but had yet to attend the two day training course. The other was a newly qualified solicitor considered by the guardian to have advocacy skills suitable for the particular case.

The majority of the solicitors in the study were supportive of the present system whereby the guardian appointed them. They acknowledged that guardians needed to be able to appoint solicitors that they could get on with so that the partnership could flourish. The guardian would rely on the legal skills of the solicitor, so the solicitor would rely on the social work skills of the guardian.

'Yes the guardian appoints. I am not happy with a court appointment system. The guardian and solicitor need to have a close working relationship. The solicitor will of course be guided by the guardian because it is the guardian who has the social work background.'

But appointment by the guardian was also problematic for the solicitor's independence:

'I do not like the guardian appointment system . . . There is a level of patronage involved which I find unhealthy. It can lead to pacts . . . You handle the case by the type of guardian you have got.'

Concerns about the power guardians have over solicitors have also been raised by panel managers (Faulkner 1995). Individual guardians and solicitors varied in their approach to visiting children. In care order, contact and discharge applications most guardians visited the children alone initially and later introduced the solicitor to the child. Guardians subsequently visited alone or with the solicitor. In applications for secure accommodation orders the approach appeared quite different. Three of the four guardians visited with the solicitor. It was thought this reflected the professionals' concern for safety whilst distance was also a factor – the units were many miles from the professionals' area.

Some solicitors always attended visits with the guardian, some did so initially when the guardian would introduce the solicitor to the child, some later visited on their own. One male guardian referred to his own concern about visiting children on their own.

> 'There were in fact a number of reasons for that [seeing children with solicitors]. One of which was because of the concerns of sexual abuse. I became aware that I could be vulnerable to allegations being made, at least I thought it was best . . . that the solicitor was there to protect me, not only the child.'

Concern for the safety of the professionals was an issue in one of the study cases, a discharge of a care order. The young girl in question had a male solicitor and a male guardian because the original guardian, a female, had been physically attacked by one of the child's relatives.

One solicitor stated clearly that the purpose of the visit to the young person was to determine how the solicitor should conduct the case.

> 'Should I be putting the child's views to the court? But then they conflict with the guardian's and should the child be entitled to have those views put forward? And that is one of the reasons why you have got to see the older children.'

Another solicitor in the study referred to the importance of remembering who the client is:

> '. . . you have to make clear time and time again to almost everybody in the case that you are the solicitor for the child . . .'

In practice, however, the majority of solicitors take their instructions from the guardian ad litem. Only if there is a conflict between what the young person wants and what the guardian is recommending to the court, and the child is deemed to be competent, must a solicitor take instruction from the child direct. There were no cases of solicitors separately representing young people in the study. Five of the solicitors and guardians could recall one or two cases of separate representation but most admitted that they were increasingly few and far between. As one solicitor said:

'. . . it would usually be a discussion between myself and the guardian . . . a number of the guardians . . . we would tend to, sort of co-work as long as we can, so that if we are talking about a split, we're talking a split at the end really, in terms of the court proceedings. And I don't think I have actually had one . . . where there has been splits. Because the concept of welfare . . . they sort of . . . they overlap . . .'

One guardian drew attention to the fact that the solicitor and guardian should continue to work together as long as was practicable even though the child disagreed with the guardian. This would ensure that the professionals remained aware of the same developments, which would reduce the risk of young people playing one professional off against another.

'And especially with teenagers, I try to see the child with the solicitor . . . most of the time and we try very hard to keep it together as a team right up until near the very end and then if there is going to be any divergence between me and the child, at least the solicitor has all the information I have got and vice versa. It actually stops the child trying to play one off against the other. Teenagers are very good at telling slightly different stories to different people.'

Taking instructions from the young person could raise further dilemmas for the solicitor. One solicitor involved in the study referred to a previous case where she had taken direct instructions from a teenager and agreed to keep the young person's confidence:

'. . . and I've given her every opportunity to say, you know, that she hates this man and she doesn't want to be with him and she's never said a thing. Only on one occasion has she expressed some concern. And she said I was going to tell you but I don't want you to tell anybody else. So I haven't. I didn't tell the guardian because that was the agreement. I was then telephoned by her mother's solicitor to say that she had told her mother . . . that she had told me something and he was ringing to confirm what she had told me. And I said, "I'm saying nothing because it's confidential between me and her."'

The Solicitors Family Law Association advise that client confidentiality is at the individual solicitor's discretion, subject to the Law Society's Guidelines on confidentiality (SFLA 1995). Brasse has taken this further, highlighting the fact that a solicitor may take instruction from the child direct but the client–solicitor confidentiality is not necessarily applicable if there are child protection issues (Brasse 1996).

Appointing barristers

There was only one barrister appointed in the cases in the interview sample. The majority of the cases remained in the family proceedings court and all

were uncontested at the final hearing. Eleven solicitors said that they generally did their own advocacy work. Six mentioned the undertaking given, as
a Children Panel member, to remain in control of the case and believed that
guardians preferred solicitors to do their own advocacy. Eight referred to
the need to employ a barrister where the case was lengthy and the solicitor
was unable to commit such time to one case. Only three gave complexity as a
reason to employ a barrister.

Solicitors from the Children Panel often do their own advocacy in public
law cases even though barristers may be employed by the other parties. Two
solicitors confirmed that they had already acted as advocates in High Court
cases. Six solicitors did, however, refer to the judicial preference for barristers in the higher courts and agreed that they would not act as advocate if
this prejudiced the outcome in any way.

The following two quotes from solicitors highlight their awareness of the
judicial preference for barristers:

> 'I do my own advocacy in the magistrates' court. If in county court and the case
> is complex or there is a time issue then I will appoint a barrister. Judges, locally,
> still want barristers.'

> 'I do my own advocacy in the magistrates' court. In county court it would
> depend on the length of the case. I would probably get a barrister in. Judges are
> prejudiced against solicitors doing work. Judges can make life difficult for
> solicitor advocates acting in person, no barrister. Yet a lot of barristers are not
> necessarily experienced in child cases. They are not specialists. A barrister not
> following the case could be a problem.'

Many judges will have trained as barristers themselves and favour their
style of advocacy. Indeed, negative comments were made in *Re B.* (1996) by
Thorpe J. about local authorities who are represented only by solicitors in
care cases. There may also be concern that the court needs to be able to
recruit new judges who have had substantial experience as barristers in this
work.

Seven guardians stated that they preferred solicitors to continue to advocate in court rather than employing a barrister. For example:

> 'Quite a lot of solicitors will advocate in court. This is good. The solicitor knows
> the case. The solicitor has seen and knows the child so it is good for the solicitor
> to advocate.'

> 'Unfortunately a barrister may end up reading the case on the train the morn-
> ing of the hearing and may miss a subtle point whereas the solicitor will have
> been in the know.'

Other guardians in the study identified other factors necessitating the
appointment of a barrister. As with solicitors, guardians were aware that

appointing a barrister may have more to do with the court system than the needs of the individual case:

'Barristers. Yes, . . . I will separate it out and insist on a barrister if the case goes to county court and is contested. Judges prefer this. They prefer to see a barrister involved.'

'Solicitors for children are good advocates but the criteria in having a barrister may be, 'Who is the Judge?' The Old Boy Network may be an important consideration here. If the solicitor is not going to get recognised as much, then get a barrister if it is going to affect the case for the child.'

Appointing barristers could also have disadvantages. One guardian reflected:

'In a case I have at present there are five barristers but there have been difficulties because of the barristers having other cases, other commitments. The case has been adjourned because of the barristers and then the judge couldn't hear it all in one go! The effect on the family and the others involved is that they have poor images of barristers and judges. They feel that priority is that of barristers and their court time and the focus on the issues of the case is lost.'

If barristers are to be instructed because solicitors are not able to tie themselves up for a lengthy case, then barristers must be able to guarantee that they will deal with the case. The CAAC, amongst others, has suggested that there should be a specialist panel for barristers along the lines of the Children Panel for solicitors. Barristers specialising in child care work would be listed as such and would give undertakings to see the case through. The Family Law Bar Association continues to oppose such suggestions and has indicated that the Bar Council would not be receptive to such an idea (CAAC 1997, 16). A specialist panel would also help solicitors and guardians select a suitable barrister.

In the study six solicitors felt that whilst they had sufficient knowledge to know which barristers specialised in Children Act cases locally, problems did arise for them when the case was 'out of the area'.

'Locally I know which barristers specialise and can choose accordingly. Generally I get the barrister that I wanted. I would encourage a panel for barristers because off patch I don't know barristers at present, and at times I need culturally appropriate child care barristers.'

'I would like to do more of my own advocacy. There is no problem, well, it is getting better. I would welcome a Children Panel for barristers. Yes that would be good. Family barristers are not necessarily child care barristers. Their level of expertise is wanting. When I need a barrister, for example I have a case in the High Court, then I contact a barrister friend, that I knew at university, and ask for advice.'

Most guardians felt that a panel for barristers would be advantageous because barristers would need extra training to be on the panel. The

minority of guardians who were unsure about such a development referred
to their own preference for solicitors as advocates because the solicitor knew
the case and the child. If a barrister was to be instructed most guardians
relied on the solicitor to select someone appropriate:

> 'I leave the choice of barrister to the solicitor. Most solicitors in county court
> like to run the cases themselves but time can be a problem for solicitors in-
> volved in long cases so they may need to consider having a barrister.'

But a few made decisions about this with the solicitor:

> 'The solicitor and I together choose an experienced barrister. I have had experi-
> ence of observing barristers over a number of years. They need to take on
> board the anti-adversarial stance in child care work. Not just in court. The
> barrister can affect things negatively. In the waiting area the barrister can come
> along with an adversarial air. There is a training need here for barristers. They
> need to appreciate the difference. There is a gap.'

Guardians commented that under the current system a different barrister
may turn up on the day and also noted that a barrister, who was not a
specialist in Children Act cases, instructed by another party, may, through
ignorance, disrupt the running of the whole case.

> 'Solicitors know which barrister to choose. I have not had a bad experience
> although on one case we did not end up with the barrister we wanted on the
> day. A panel for barristers would be helpful. In one of my cases the local
> authority instructed a barrister who did not know anything of child care work.
> It was very obvious.'

> 'Some solicitors do have their favourites. I like to be involved in the choosing
> and I will remind the solicitor of this early on. I think a Child Panel of barristers
> would be good. In one hearing the parents were separately represented by two
> criminal barristers who then turned up at the care proceedings. Neither had
> any idea about the care side. It was obvious that their minds were still on
> outstanding issues in criminal matters and not on the interests of the child.
> They were adversarial and obstructive. One kept arguing against the order
> because he did not want his client to lose parental responsibility. He did not
> appreciate this is not lost. In the end the parents pleaded guilty to the criminal
> charges and this had implications for the child. The care order was finally
> made by agreement but the solicitor for the child has now told me that the
> barristers want to appeal the care order. The solicitor and I refer to them as
> Tweedledum and Tweedledee.'

The chain of representation

Introducing a new professional, who has not experienced the developments
of the case as the solicitor has, may be problematic in itself. A solicitor noted:

'I have had my instructions ignored by a barrister. I do not like instructing barristers at short notice. They need to be made aware of issues and to be clear about them.'

Another professional involved in the case further distances the young person from the representation. The child's wishes and feelings may become distorted as the chain becomes longer, particularly if new members do not hear directly from the child. The child tells the guardian who tells the solicitor who tells the barrister who tells the court. An analogy may be drawn with the experiences of a guardian who had difficulty when seeking information about a local authority's application. The guardian worried that the information became distorted as it passed through various people. He explained:

'. . . where there has been more information, I have found that sometimes by the time it's got from the court clerk to the admin. office and then from the admin. office to me, it's a bit like Chinese whispers . . . So there's certain things that are hyped up or left out . . . I'd much rather receive the paperwork that the local authority has submitted to the court.'

When the solicitors appoint barristers, a trainee solicitor, a legal executive or a legal secretary may act as the firm's representative in court. None of these people are likely to have met the young person. Consequently, the chain is lengthened and the child further distanced from the process. If the guardian could not attend the hearing there would be no representative at court who had met the child and heard the child's wishes at first hand. This occurred in one of the study cases.

The guardian was unable to attend the final hearing because of another case in the High Court. The solicitor attended the court on behalf of the 11 year old child who was not present. The solicitor had not seen the child during these proceedings. There were major developments in the case during the proceedings; the child ran away from his placement – this led to the local authority changing its perspective and to the guardian filing an additional report. The child was not represented in court by anyone he had spoken to about his wishes, nor did he have the opportunity afterwards to speak to a representative who had attended the hearing on his behalf.

Although the research did not include a survey of barristers, a leading child law barrister who spoke to the researchers stated that he hardly ever sees children and did not consider this as part of his role. Rather, he relied on instructions from solicitors. This approach was confirmed by the majority of solicitors and guardians in the study who did not see a need for barristers to meet children. This contrasts sharply with their expectations and practices where children are represented by solicitors. This point will be returned to shortly.

Five guardians said that they would feel uncomfortable about introducing yet another stranger, albeit a professional, into the children's lives. They were concerned that this would be a negative development and would confuse young people.

> 'I am not keen for barristers to see the child. It is not significant, not beneficial. Bearing in mind a child's age and understanding, it would just be another stranger.'

> 'It is not important for barristers to see the child unless the child is going to be at court. Barristers will perhaps see the child before the hearing. There are not many cases where children come to court.'

> 'No, the barristers that I know would not meet the child. I do not think there is a need for them to meet the child. They have nothing to gain from this. They will get their information from the solicitor and the guardian . . . If an older child is pushing to meet the barrister then maybe I would consider it but it has not happened to date.'

This last quote betrays the adult focus which is endemic. *'They have nothing to gain from this'* is said in relation to the barrister and not to the child. No consideration was given, by this or other respondents, to whether the child would benefit from meeting their barrister.

Whilst guardians and solicitors accepted that barristers do not need to meet the young people they represent, they asserted that there are benefits for the child's solicitor to see the child and hear the wishes of the child. There appears to be an expectation that solicitors should see all children, even babies.

> 'I will always see the child, even a baby because even babies have characteristics that you need to be aware of.'

> 'Yes I see all children including a baby. One reason for this is that it is important to check the placement where the child is living.'

The above quotes highlight that for these solicitors representing children was not an 'at arm's length' activity but one that required the solicitor to take on board the characteristics of the child and to see the child in context. For barristers representation was attending court on behalf of a child. The guardians confirmed this view:

> 'Barristers don't see the child. Once on a secure accommodation order case a barrister attended who was opposing the order on behalf of the child. I say child, the child was a young person of 16 years. I was there with the young person who the barrister was representing. The barrister came along and introduced himself to me and totally ignored the young person, the client, who stood with me. The young person took exception to this. Barristers should introduce themselves, make themselves known to the young person. You need to point this out to them.'

But a change in approach may be coming, as one guardian recounted following a presentation at a conference of the National Association of Guardians ad Litem and Reporting Officers.

'No, I have not been aware of any barrister seeing a child or asking to see a child. Having said that I was at a NAGALRO conference last week and there was a barrister there who actually said that he would like to meet more children but he never gets asked. I have to say this made me think about my practice and about the pros and cons of barristers meeting children.'

In the study cases only one barrister was appointed and this was to represent a 16 year old girl who was the mother of a baby subject to care proceedings. The young person was already the subject of an application for a secure accommodation order. The solicitor arranged for the girl to meet with the barrister in conference and the girl attended the care order proceedings.

'[The barrister] met her at one hearing . . . we were going to have a conference with her prior to the final hearing . . . There was never any question of [the child] not going to court . . . with [the child] we had a meeting before we went to court . . . we always assumed that she would come to court. Because I mean, she was . . . you know, it was a question about her own daughter. So I think it was different. 'Cause she was actually a parent . . .'

The solicitor asserted that the girl had been fully involved. However, in explaining the developments in the case to the researcher, she began to acknowledge that this had been because the child was a parent. The child's involvement was not in her own right, but as a mother of her child. The solicitor continued to discuss the irony of the situation:

'And I think, you know, it would be wrong . . . I suppose . . . double standards really, isn't it? Saying that you should come to court because it's your child, we're making decisions . . . But if you're a child and it's your future being decided, we don't really need you at court . . .'

GUARDIANS AND CHILDREN, YOUNG PEOPLE AND GUARDIANS

Once appointed, guardians contacted the child through their parents or foster carers and arranged to visit them. The majority of visits took place at the young person's current home and for children of school age, after school. All guardians saw the child at least twice, and three guardians made over five visits to the child (Table 1a).

Some guardians made only two visits to children when applications involved renewal of secure accommodation applications or where the local

Table 1a: Meetings between the young person and their guardian

<2	2–3	4–5	5+	Total
–	4	9	3	16*

* Where children were involved in proceedings with siblings only one child from the group is included in this table.

authority sought to discharge a care order. Other applications, like those for care orders, involved more visits. Visits ranged from two to seven and varied in length according to what the guardian and the child had to say.

Where cases last many months guardians tended to make more visits, partly because of changes in the child's life and partly to keep the child informed.

Children commented about the numbers and frequency of the visits from their guardian but they had different views about this.

'I didn't want to see her that much anyway. It just gets on my nerves. Well it was OK about once every three weeks. But if she was coming every week it would really get on my nerves.'

'She didn't come often enough, only about three times . . .'

'She came a bit too many times – sometimes nearly 20 minutes going over old ground.'

'I've had her for ages, I've had her ever since I've been in secure.'

All the children interviewed were able to give an explanation of the work of a guardian; these varied in depth but were all broadly accurate.

'He writes and sends it to the court, he writes what I say.'

'Looking after the child while a court case is going on . . .'

'The job of the guardian is to say what you are feeling. She said exactly what I wanted her to say.'

'A person who talks about things to you . . . Do you like living in these foster houses?'

And from a young person who was the subject of repeated applications for secure accommodation orders:

'Once you get elected to a guardian they stay . . . for years . . .'

Some guardians preferred to take children away from where they were living on some visits. This, they said, enabled children to feel free to talk about their wishes and feelings without fear of being overheard by others in the household. On the other hand, this practice did cause concern:

> 'I'm very iffy about taking children out much because I think the whole ethos is almost telling them what to do, what you have spent your whole life telling other children what not to do. You know you say, "Don't go with strangers." So what do we do, we take a child out.'

One guardian acknowledged that he did take children out if it was difficult to talk to them on their own but he did not approve of trips to places such as McDonald's. He felt that many parents would be unable to pay for such trips. Guardians were giving the wrong messages with such 'treats' and hence were abusing their power in behaving in this way.

Another guardian felt that 'over friendly' guardians were abusing their professional position, since their role was a short-term one, ending with the end of the court proceedings. He felt that children would be confused about the messages they were getting, particularly so because they were vulnerable children and were susceptible to those who showed them kindness.

However, for some children the guardian and the solicitor were the only visitors they had other than a social worker. Trips out often turned into treats with visits to McDonald's, Burger King, or even to a bird sanctuary. A number of solicitors and guardians bought the children small gifts. These included a chocolate orange, sweets, cigarettes, a football, a football scarf, a ring, and a small toy lizard. Some children referred to these treats when asked to describe what they liked about their guardian.

> 'He takes me out.'

> 'She buys my fags.'

> 'We went to McDonalds.'

Other children focused on what the guardian said or did:

> 'The way she listened.'

> 'She was funny.'

> 'She always brought toys . . . she's got this weird way of acting . . . speaking to teddies.'

The majority of young people stated that they felt that they could trust their guardians. They said that they trusted their guardian to tell the court what it was they wanted. This was the case both for young people who attended court and for those who did not.

SOLICITORS AND CHILDREN, YOUNG PEOPLE AND SOLICITORS

Whilst all the children and young people in the study were able to describe the role of the guardian, some appeared to be confused about the role of their solicitor. Three thought it was the same as the guardian, two had no idea what a solicitor did. This confusion could be understood given that the majority did not attend court and so did not see their solicitor in action. Those young people with clearest perceptions were older and had attended a court hearing. All four young people subject to applications for secure accommodation orders had attended court and had heard their solicitor speak in court. There was an expectation amongst representatives and the court that the young people would attend secure accommodation hearings.

Quotes from children who attended court about the role of the solicitor:

'Talks for you, doesn't she, in court.'

'The solicitors are more to do with the paperwork and the legal side of it . . . they speak for you at court.'

'A solicitor's job is to protect you and if you don't want to say anything in court they can represent you.'

Some quotes from children who did not attend court about the role of the solicitor:

'I really don't know 'cause I didn't see her that much . . .'

'Quick.'

'They are just meant to say what I think about what I am doing and where I want to stay and all that.'

'Well . . . telling the magistrates what I want and don't want.'

'Roughly the same as [the guardian].'

Guidance to solicitors about seeing the child emphasises the need to build up a relationship gradually and suggests that several unhurried meetings will be required to establish a working relationship (Liddle 1992, 12). Solicitors were often introduced to the child by the guardian and subsequently visited the child alone or with the guardian as they (or the guardian) thought fit.

'I would want to be introduced because just to turn up out of nowhere, when they may have difficulty conceptualising the whole thing let alone the role of the solicitor and *their* solicitor. I would like to go and be introduced and discuss it with the guardian.'

'Normally . . . I see them together [with the guardian] to start with and then separately if necessary later, possibly if we are talking about a teenager then I may well see the child separately right from the start to formulate my own opinions really.'

Visiting with the guardian helped solicitors who had difficulty establishing rapport with their child clients.

'I take a back seat because I'm not trained in the talking to children techniques that guardians are. If it's a younger child and I'm not expecting to take instructions directly I don't think it's particularly helpful to get involved with the child. So I tend to observe.'

'It could have been a darn sight harder if she [the guardian] hadn't been [there]. I mean, I died on my feet on the first interview. I don't think I'd have got through the door on the second one if she hadn't been there.'

The guardian's skill in communicating with children helped the solicitor.

'The guardian can ease the solicitor into their role with the child. [The guardian] tells me a bit more about the child before I visit, such as, what football team the child supports or the latest group they like. Then I will have to do my homework, such as watch Top of the Pops and get in the know. This helps my credibility with the child, particularly with difficult teenagers. [The guardian] will give me this feedback.'

Sylvia's solicitor told her at her second visit that she would not see her for a week because she was going away on holiday. Sylvia had had very few holidays and had never been abroad. Her face lit up and she asked her solicitor to tell her about her holidays. Her solicitor explained that she was going somewhere exotic. Sylvia urged her solicitor to tell her more about her holidays and she consented, provided Sylvia listened to her for a few minutes while she talked about the proceedings at court. Sylvia agreed and listened quietly as her solicitor talked about the local authority care plan and the guardian report. When the solicitor had finished Sylvia begged her to talk about her holidays. She was enthralled with what she heard and giggled with delight. The solicitor (and the researcher) laughed too.

When the researcher interviewed the solicitor some weeks later she asked her about Sylvia and whether the solicitor had decided that she was competent. Her solicitor replied that she had decided that she was not competent. She explained:

'She wasn't in her . . . basically in her . . . understanding. In her general attitude . . . talk about the case. What she wanted to know about the case . . . I'd represented a girl who was probably 12 months older and there were chasms between them. Her wanting to know what was going on . . . indicated that she really had a far greater understanding. And really I mean the second interview just itself showed that for Sylvia it didn't have any major significance.'

Two solicitors did not see their child client, two others met the child only once, very briefly, for 10 minutes or less (Table 1b). In Clark's study far more solicitors had not seen their child clients. Only one-third of children had been seen by their solicitor; half of those who were not seen (14) were aged 8 years or older (Clark 1995, 93; 1995a). Half the children, in the study reported here, saw their solicitors only in the company of the guardian. Not all children found such joint visits helpful:

'We didn't see much of [the solicitor] anyway, once . . . she didn't really find out much. She's only seen us with [the guardian].'

Arrangements to visit young people were rarely made directly with children. Solicitors contacted carers to fix an appointment with the child. Court hearings took priority, solicitors sometimes had to alter appointments or they arrived late from court. Solicitors, like guardians, generally saw children where they were living, after school, but children who were the subject of secure accommodation applications were also seen at court.

When children's opinions were wanted the issues were often approached obliquely without explaining the background to the child. For example, Edward's solicitor visited him shortly before the final hearing at court; he was keen to ensure that he knew where Edward wanted to live and so he asked him this. The next day the researcher spoke with the solicitor on the telephone. The solicitor explained that he had received a call from Edward's social worker asking him about his visit to Edward the day before. Edward's behaviour had become quite disruptive after the solicitor's visit and his carers had had difficulty calming him down. The social worker asked the solicitor if he had said anything that may have upset Edward. The solicitor in turn asked the researcher whether Edward appeared upset by the solicitor's questioning. The solicitor did not believe that his questions had led to Edward's outburst.

Solicitors representing children receive little training about how to relate to children, yet children involved in care proceedings are often the most vulnerable of all children. Many solicitors learn to relate to children by

Table 1b: Meetings between the young person and their solicitor

0	1–2	3–4	5 or more	Not known	Total
2	6	4	2	2	16*

* Where children were involved in proceedings with siblings only one child from the group is included in this table.

experience but some solicitors in the study indicated that they had little confidence in their ability to speak to children.

When a solicitor had found it difficult to establish rapport he or she might cease to visit the child. Some solicitors felt that there was no real purpose in their meeting the child.

> 'Because [the guardian] had spent a lot of time with the child and they were happy with her. And I felt it was inappropriate to then put them with some-body they didn't know, they didn't really want to see, who's asking them just the same questions that everybody else had asked them. And they're fed up to the back teeth with being asked.'

Fewer visits were made in secure accommodation applications and in cases of discharge of care orders; most of these involved solicitors who had acted for the child previously. They were completed in the shortest time. Conversely, where proceedings lasted for many months solicitors made more visits.

Most of the children whose meetings with guardians and solicitors were observed, related more strongly to one of their representatives. When this happened the other representative tended to play a more limited part, rely-ing on their colleague. Solicitors sometimes took the leading role with older children. Children were not always happy with their limited involvement with their solicitor.

> 'I would have liked to see him a bit more. I know how many times I saw him. Twice. [I would have liked] to get to know him a bit more. He's busy. He had to go to court.'

> 'I've only seen her once or twice . . . I've even forgotten what she looks like . . . [my carer] did most [of the explaining] . . . She didn't really come often which I feel she should have done . . . I would have told her why I had run off and all that.'

When solicitors met their child clients they usually made sure that they had their telephone number, often by giving them a business card.

> 'I give them the ordinary business card and I make sure they have my home number . . . I think it is quite important that they have a means of communica-tion . . . it's not used often.'

Most of the children recalled this in interview but only a few older chil-dren had attempted to contact their solicitor.

> 'Well I put in the letter, if he needed to talk to me he could always get in touch with me. I think you always say that but they never do, I have never had anybody come back.'

Some solicitors wrote to older children either to tell them when they would be visiting or to confirm the outcome of the case and say goodbye.

'I wrote to him . . . that depends on their age and understanding and the significance of the letter and whether they can understand it. I think letters are really nice to have if you can follow what is happening, if it doesn't frighten you.'

Even younger children very much liked receiving letters, particularly if they were addressed to them. Most children had kept their letters.

'But I know I definitely got it on a school day . . . It came through the post when I was at school and I asked [carer] if he could read it out to me.'

Letters were important even if their contents had to be explained by others, a point recognised by two solicitors who wrote to children with the hope that information in the letter would later be useful to them.

'It is right that I should if there has been some draconian sort of order, if they don't understand it then, then at least they have got the letter later.'

If letters for children were sent to carers it was not always clear that children had seen them. Some children whose solicitors did not write to them were disappointed. One child, Charles, described a solicitor as 'someone who writes letters to other people'. It was disempowering to have to get information about these proceedings secondhand, especially if you knew that adults involved had had letters from their solicitors.

'Well it could have been, yeah really, then instead of [my carer] telling me everything I could have read it for myself.'

William was aware that his solicitor was the only solicitor to visit the secure accommodation unit. He said that the other young people could not understand why his solicitor made the effort to see him when they only saw their solicitors at court. This perception reflected the significance that having a Children Panel solicitor had for William. The other teenagers had criminal lawyers.

TALKING TO CHILDREN AND YOUNG PEOPLE

Although both guardians and solicitors were clear that the children's wishes were important, some were less concerned about discussing with children the details of what had happened to them or giving explanations of the current processes and decisions. Being child-focused and allowing the child to take the lead sometimes meant that matters like going to court or even reading the report were only addressed if the child raised them. However, it is important to emphasise that children are only able to raise issues which they are aware of. Some children were not aware that they had any options about attending court or reading the guardian's report. It was not always clear that children knew enough to ask questions or were genuinely being given opportunities to do so (Winn Oakley 1998a).

Occasionally children's opinions were only sought in the presence of carers, the situation which inhibited Carl from telling his guardian that he was not happy remaining with his mother. Siblings were not always seen individually, which made it difficult for them to give their own perspective or even to concentrate. Children did not like this.

'It would have been better because [younger sibling] is always leaping about and making noises.'

'[the solicitor] didn't really talk to us . . . She would have got to know us better if it was one person at a time.'

The ways both guardians and solicitors spoke to children also indicated a reluctance to get too involved because of their time-limited relationship with the child and concern that children would be upset because of what had been said to them. As one representative noted:

'At the end of the day we are not there to fully investigate the case and we are not there to get a confession or whatever out of the child or even for the child to say what has happened . . . I think it almost verges on abuse to question the child closely about what has happened if the child has been abused.'

Conflict

The solicitors all acknowledged that their relationship with the guardian and the child changed if the young person was giving instructions directly. Yet despite their experience and specialism in child care work – the solicitors shared over 100 years of panel expertise between them – they had little experience representing the child separately. Most could recall no more than one or two cases where this had occurred. This was also true for the guardians. There were no cases in the sample where the solicitor identified a conflict of interest between a competent child and the guardian; consequently all the solicitors took their instructions from the guardian. The solicitors' ways of working appeared to avoid the possibility of conflict arising or becoming apparent. They spent little time with the young person alone, or ensuring that the young person was properly informed about their role and had confidence in them. They did not generally spend time going through the guardian's report, and some only saw the child early in the investigations before the guardian's position had become clear. Solicitors were aware that conflict with the guardian might simply weaken the child's case, and because the magistrates held guardians in high regard, the child was unlikely to succeed in getting their way in the face of opposition from the guardian.

> 'I have to say in the magistrates' court if you are with the guardians you feel that you are sitting on the right hand side of God. The impressions the magistrates have is that if the guardians say something, who are they to question their judgement.'

Where conflict did arise, for example where a child did not want to be in a secure placement but the case for this was strong, solicitors advised children against opposing the application on the basis that compliance would be viewed positively and would lead to increased privileges. In one of the secure accommodation cases in the study, both the guardian and the solicitor were in agreement that an order should be made. The young man concerned explained how his solicitor told him that another order would be of benefit to him:

> '. . . I didn't want an order . . . I was getting bored . . . my solicitor thought there should be an order . . . he said it would be best and in the end I agreed . . . I will oppose it next time.'

The practice of managing adult clients in similar ways is well known (McConville et al 1994). Similarly, if an older child had very strong views about their future, the guardian might reconsider their recommendation. One solicitor recounted a case where this had occurred:

> 'The guardian felt that [the child's] views were so much an intricate part of her welfare that an order was not going to be successful.'

Avoiding conflict at the early stage also ensured that the guardian had the support of the solicitor for most of the preparation of the case as the guardians quoted on p. 63 remarked.

Where children and guardians have conflicting instructions for the solicitor, the child needs legal representation. It is not clear that this will always be best provided in cases of late separations by the solicitor who is already acting in the case. One solicitor had had the experience of being approached directly by a child seeking representation having lost confidence in the solicitor originally chosen by the guardian.

The final hearing was uncontested in all of the sample cases, although it was clear that some had involved considerable behind the scenes negotiations with the local authority about the care plan and that parental opposition had withered during the course of the proceedings.

Goodbye visits

Most of the children and young people did not attend court and so had to rely on an adult explaining the court outcome. Sometimes children did not see their social workers, guardians or solicitors for some days or weeks afterwards and had to wait to be told officially what had happened.

The aunt of a child referred to this point during her nephew's interview.

> 'With them all it was like they seemed to leave everything to me. No one came back to tell him.'

The guardians generally made a 'goodbye visit' to the child after the hearing and used this opportunity to make certain that the child knew that the proceedings were over, what had been decided and that there would be no more visits from the guardian. Most visits were made within a couple of weeks of the hearing. Edward's guardian delayed the visit for a number of weeks in the hope that she could see him settled in his new placement, but finally visited him in his temporary foster home. In some cases the social worker had said that they would tell the child the details of the case. Where children had returned or remained at home contrary to the guardian's recommendation, guardians said that they felt uncomfortable about visiting them after the proceedings and might not do so.

Two guardians referred to past cases where they had been unable to return to see the children. In one case where no care order had been made, the parents made it clear that they would not agree to visits by either the guardian or the solicitor and no visit was made. A panel manager hoped that professionals would work together and that social workers would assist guardians in visiting children. It appeared that abandoning the visit was sometimes easier than 'working together', even where the child was subject to a care order.

> 'I didn't because the father had been so horrible when I went, I thought I am not putting myself through this again. But the child knew what she wanted . . .'

In the other case, a care order was made and the child was placed at home, the parents refused to allow either the guardian or the solicitor to visit the child, and the local authority would not support the guardian ad litem's attempt to visit.

In addition to the two solicitors who did not see the child at all, six
solicitors did not return to see the child after the final hearing. Goodbyes
were said at the visit prior to the final hearing or at court if children attended. The following quote highlights reasons for this:

'It depends. Not if the child was young and I was not taking instructions
because I would hope that I would not be a significant person in their lives any
way . . . Sometimes yes, if the children are older and they want to discuss what
it means to them and what their future position is and what their rights are
about the order . . . yes.'

Four solicitors returned to visit the young person after the final hearing.
Two of these were adamant that they would always visit the child after the
final hearing to explain to them the outcome and discuss other issues.
William's solicitor said that he always visited the young people after the
hearing, certainly if they were older, to debrief them.

'I always go . . . I mean, they always know when it is in court . . . I mean
obviously we are talking about older . . . older children. I would always go
back and tell them the outcome. Even when the outcome is certain . . . I would
tend to go back for a de-briefing like . . . what was it like then?'

He continued:

'There are messages to give about what happened at court, make sure they
understand that. Secondly [if] a care order has been made, they need to know
and may need you again if they want you, so again you spend time with them.
Then there are other issues such as Criminal Injuries Compensation, by and
large you tax local authority on that and say, 'You are going to do that aren't
you?' . . . It has to be done and there again, depending on the case and the age
appropriateness of the child, they may need to know and you can tell them to
get back in touch with you . . .'

For solicitors 'goodbye visits' were an opportunity to ensure not only that
the child understood what had happened but also that he or she knew that
they could contact the solicitor about other issues in the future. Three solicitors confirmed that they passed on business cards to the young people when
they met. One solicitor used the 'goodbye' visit to ensure that the young
people still had the card. If they needed another one then this would be
passed on at the final visit. One firm of solicitors had researched the design
of their business cards with teenagers in mind. It was brightly coloured and
resembled an access card:

'Yes you see it looks like a cheque card . . . and it is just that little bit different.'

This solicitor hoped that the teenagers would continue to carry it around
with them, and have it at hand for future contact. He admitted that the card

had originally been designed for teenagers involved in criminal proceedings but his firm had since had some printed for Children Act work too. A business card could be important for the child, enabling him or her to contact the solicitor in the future. It could also be important for the solicitor, leading to more work if the child got into trouble or needed a lawyer for other reasons.

CONCLUSION

Practice has developed haphazardly from individual guardians' views about what is the right way to go about being a child's guardian ad litem. Solicitors have tended to follow the guardians' lead because of their own inexperience and dependence upon the guardians for appointment. Young people have limited ability to steer the process because of their experience and age. They are further handicapped by the limited knowledge they are provided with and by views and practices that elevate their protection from the proceedings over their participation in them.

There was a strong overtone of paternalism in much of what the guardians said about their work. Guardians were also concerned that they should not trespass into, or take responsibility for, work which the social services department should do.

6

GETTING REPRESENTATION

For the guardian, the process of acting for a child or young person in care proceedings usually starts with a call from the panel administrator to check availability and discuss taking on a new case. Although each child a guardian represents is an individual and each case is different, appointment sets a process in train with which the guardian is very familiar.

There is no single way in which children and young people come to know that court proceedings about them have been started or that a guardian ad litem has been appointed for them. They may learn about the proceedings without experiencing any other changes in their lives. Proceedings may appear to be just a process to formalise an arrangement which is already well established. Where this is the case the proceedings may scarcely impinge on the child's life, the only obvious signs being a few visits from the professionals, the social worker, the guardian ad litem and solicitor. Charles was made the subject of a care order when he was at infant school. He continued to live with his mother and her partner, and active social work involvement with Charles' family ceased relatively quickly. Charles had not seen a social worker for some time. The local authority's application to discharge his care order when he was 9 years old passed almost unnoticed. Charles met the guardian but had little memory of the visits.

But even where proceedings are not accompanied by changes in carer or residence, learning that proceedings have been started can cause considerable disruption. The mention of court proceedings may itself be a cause of anxiety. The news that his mother, whom he had not seen for seven years, was applying for a contact order came as a shock to Tom. His foster carer was clearly anxious about the proceedings. Tom was angry and worried about what he saw as a threat to his home life.

For other children and young people it is only too obvious that major changes are occurring before the proceedings are started, with escalating difficulties in relationships, deteriorating care and abuse and possibly separation from parents. Even so, the precipitating incident and the proceedings may come out of the blue. Children and young people entering public care are having to come to terms with removal from home and placement in unfamiliar surroundings, to establish relationships with new carers and their children, and to settle into new routines when the proceedings are started.

Sylvia's single mother died suddenly; her father had recently been released following a prison sentence for sexual offences against her. Sylvia spent a few weeks staying with different relatives but none felt able to offer her a home; the local authority arranged a temporary foster placement and applied for a care order. Edward had been living with his mother and stepfather and their young children. Social services were involved because of concerns about Edward's care and his behaviour. Apparently without warning, Edward's mother left home telling no-one where she was going; Edward's stepfather asked the social services department to look after Edward. Edward was placed with a foster family some miles from his former home.

Although children and young people in the care system, particularly those in residential care, are often well versed in the language of the public care system, its processes, intricacies and vocabulary are not part of common knowledge for adults or children. Unless children or young people remember previously being involved in care proceedings, being told a guardian ad litem has been appointed, that proceedings have been started or that a court will decide what is to happen is unlikely to convey much meaning. They hear that something else is going to happen but when and what remains unclear. Courts are generally associated with wrongdoing; even law students sometimes confuse civil and criminal law. Five children spontaneously referred in their interview to thinking that they were criminals or must have done something wrong when they learnt that the local authority was bringing proceedings. Uncertainty and misunderstanding increase anxiety.

Introductions

Although the guardian ad litem may become a trusted representative, or even a friend, initially he or she is a *stranger* whose official title gives little indication of their role. Meeting the child or young person and immediately establishing a working relationship with them presents the guardian ad litem with a major challenge. The time-limited nature of the guardian's involvement and the emphasis on avoiding delay provide the impetus for getting on with the work.

> 'Soon. Usually within the week. Hopefully before [the next hearing] although it's very difficult sometimes, when you're appointed to get a visit in to the child prior to the first hearing.'

> '. . . Sometimes you have very little notice and you've got to act straight away.'

At this point, the guardian may know little about the young person and have no idea what he or she already knows.

Children and young people were not always informed in advance of their first meeting with the guardian, by their carers, by their social worker or by the guardian. This protected them from the anxiety of anticipation but meant that they were not prepared for the visit. Initial (and later meetings) were frequently arranged by telephone with carers; where letters were sent they were often addressed to carers. Children and young people were not necessarily shown them nor told of their contents. Contact with carers may help to ensure that the child or young person is available but can also mean that the first a young person knows of the guardian's appointment or visit is a ring at the door. It reinforces the view that the proceedings are something which is happening to them, rather than something they are involved in.

Some guardians worked hard to ensure the child was expecting their visit and ready to engage with them. One explained how she did this. It was her practice to write to children and young people direct in order to introduce herself. She bought greetings cards, adding her own brief message inside, setting the child a puzzle. For example, she might send a card with a picture of sweets on it and ask a 6 year old child to tell her, when she visited, how many sweets there were on the card. With older children she often chose 'Forever Friends' cards because she knew they were popular. She found that children awaited her visit and were eager to give her the answer. Sending the card gave her 'an edge', young people remembered her.

Guardians' first meeting with the child they were representing was often quite brief. Most of the guardians said that they usually used the first visit to explain who they were and what they were doing. Peter, aged 10 was shown the video *Not Alone* from the Department of Health information pack for children involved in care proceedings (DH 1995a). He was the only child in the study to have seen it. He found it rather difficult to take in at the same time as his first meeting with his guardian.

> 'It helped me a bit. I didn't understand any of it. I sat and watched it with [my guardian]. We just sat and watched it and talked about it at the end . . . It was confusing 'cause it was the first time [the guardian] came.'

Even experienced guardians might experience difficulty establishing rapport with an angry young person. One solicitor recalled:

> 'The first time [the guardian] met [a girl placed in secure accommodation] she literally spat at her and said, 'I'm not speaking to you, cause you're another social worker and I'm just a bag of shit to social services.' She didn't want anything to do with us and we traipsed up and down [to the distant secure unit] trying to build a relationship with her.'

Generally only after the guardian had established a relationship with the child would they introduce the solicitor. Although some solicitors were content to make their own arrangements to see child clients, particularly those who were older, there was a strong preference amongst solicitors in the study, and amongst guardians, for an introduction by the guardian. Solicitors stressed that the guardian could prepare them and the child for the meeting with the solicitor:

> '[The guardian ad litem] sets the groundwork so she will have seen them before and discussed with them who this next person is who she is going to bring into their lives.'

A solicitor from another part of the country explained that because she was a stranger to the child she needed the guardian to arrange an introduction. Problems arose with this approach if the guardian failed to make the appointment.

> 'It is expected that the solicitor should make arrangements via the guardian ad litem and if correspondence asking for such a meeting to be arranged is ignored this leaves the solicitor in an impossible situation as it would generally be wholly inappropriate to approach a child who is likely to have already undergone significant difficulties in their life without an appropriate introduction from the guardian ad litem.'

The guardian might tell the child that the solicitor would come with them on their next visit but such arrangements were not possible if diaries had not already been checked. Unless this happened or the guardian spoke to the child by telephone, the child's meeting with the solicitor might also come without warning.

> 'I don't normally write some letter of introduction. I don't know whether some solicitors do or not. I suppose if it was a boy of 14 or 15, or a girl, after my first visit I would probably write to confirm who I am and what I'm doing.'

Two of the 12 solicitors confirmed that it was their practice to write short introductory letters to young people before meeting them. These letters did not detail the role of the solicitor but confirmed the dates of visits. Other solicitors said that they preferred to be introduced personally to the young person by the guardian. Solicitors who made their own arrangements to visit found it convenient to rely on the foster carers:

> 'What happens is you'd always ring up the foster carer first of all to make sure they are going to be in, they haven't got football practice or whatever. And then you follow it up with a letter to say, 'I'm coming to see you on this day.' Just a reminder really. Because if you are making a child stop in when they really want to be out at football practice you're going to get nothing out of them.'

The limited information the children and young people had about their guardian and solicitor before they met them served to emphasise that these people were strangers to them. Contact by letter or telephone before the first meeting, and the provision of some basic written information, might have helped young children to prepare for the first meeting.

Information for children and young people

When the Children Act 1989 was implemented, the Department of Health published a series of brightly coloured leaflets for children and young people, including one specifically about court proceedings under the Act (DH 1991b). Amongst other things, this describes the role of the guardian ad litem and solicitor and explains in clear language the court process. The researchers have no information about the current availability and use of these leaflets; none of the children and young people in the study had copies of them.

Representation necessarily involves the representative in a two way process, finding out about the child or young person and giving him or her information about the process. The apparently simple task of providing information is fraught with difficulty. Information is not value free, it may be reassuring but can be a source of anxiety, particularly if it is difficult to understand. The guardian and solicitor have to decide what to explain and how best to do this. The child's age and stage of development are obviously important, as is the information to be imparted. More fundamentally these decisions depend on beliefs about what the child or young person should be told.

Representation by a guardian ad litem is a right except where the court is satisfied that it is not necessary in order to safeguard the child's interests (Children Act 1989, s. 41(1)). Access to information is therefore a right. Not all young people want to know about their proceedings; a children's rights perspective must also take account of the individual child's choice. Emphasis on 'the need to know' and the wish to protect children and young people can make professionals, parents and carers reluctant to tell them things. The guardian's paradigm of representation is crucial. If representation is about ensuring the court is fully aware of the child or young person's wishes and feelings, there may be relatively little which he or she needs to know. But if the guardian sees the purpose of representation as helping a young person to participate in the process, far more will be necessary.

> 'In order to participate effectively in decision making, children need accurate and truthful information. Information empowers children to make meaningful choices and sometimes adults and professionals have difficulty in allowing the child the right to information.' (Timms 1995, 178)

Providing information is recognised in the Court Rules and in professional guidance as an important element in representation for children. But provision of information is contingent on the child's maturity or understanding and depends on what the representative considers to be appropriate. The rules require the solicitor to advise the child with sufficient understanding about the contents of documents; the Solicitors Family Law Association guidance urges particular care in showing documents to children and suggests that solicitors should take advice from the guardian ad litem or other professionals involved in the case. It stresses that children should have the same respect as adult clients and recognises the importance of advice in some situations: 'A solicitor should ensure a mature child as client has sufficient information to make informed decisions' (SFLA 1995). The Court Rules require the guardian to 'give such advice to the child as is appropriate having regard to his understanding' (FPR r. 4.11(1)). This is emphasised by a statement in guidance that, 'the child should be kept informed and helped to understand the process of investigation and the reasons for the guardian's recommendation to the court' (DH and WO 1995, 15) and suggestions about how this might be monitored in the guidance on implementing the National Standards (DH 1996, 50).

Despite the guardian's professional independence and the lack of management or supervision of guardian's work, some panels develop their own ethos. The National Standards project (DH and WO 1995) encourages this with a view to ensuring that there is a coherent guardian service operating consistently in each area rather than a collection of individuals who all perform their role as guardians differently.

One outward sign of the panel's ethos is the information provided for children involved in proceedings. Work done by members of a panel to draft panel leaflets may be instrumental in formulating and agreeing a common approach which may then be developed through training. The contents of leaflets, particularly the information provided, their depth and focus, what is omitted and the way information is presented, reflect the panel members' paradigm of representation. Panels which had drafted leaflets had frequently produced two versions differing in content and style, one for children and one for young people, possibly indicating different models for representing children and young people. Expectations about the use of panel leaflets would serve to reinforce and implement the agreed approach, but the researchers were not aware of any panel which required guardians to provide leaflets for children. The fact that a panel does not have a leaflet for children may indicate that a common approach to representation has not been agreed and may also suggest that giving written information to children is not a priority of the panel. Children and young people with guardians who do not give written information have to rely on what they are told and on their memory. Where leaflets are not provided for use by panel members, individual guardians may choose to give information in writing, in a letter to the child or, more usually, by using leaflets from other panels or organisations. The fact that many guardians are members of more than one panel assists this.

Giving information

Neither of the panels in the study had prepared their own leaflet for children but some of the guardians sometimes gave children or young people the leaflet published by the charity Independent Representation for Children in Need (IRCHIN), now known as NYAS – the National Youth Advocacy Service, or other panels.

> 'Mostly with older children I will write to them. I have a letter I send. There are leaflets, I use them sometimes, I use them all the time with parents.'

Amongst those who did not use leaflets were two guardians who specifically referred to their dislike of the available leaflets and their preference for giving information verbally in order to ensure that it had been understood. This approach suggests that these guardians saw written and oral information as alternatives, and the spoken word as a better way of communicating.

The children and young people who had received leaflets all appreciated having them, even where they felt its style a little beneath them. As Amy remarked:

> 'The book was a little babyish actually. It was stick men and big writing on it.'

Carol was given written information by her guardian which included drawings and puzzles for her to complete. She told the researcher that this helped her to understand what was going on. A leaflet was 'something to keep' and could be referred to later. It was not a substitute for the individual explanation from the guardian; it might be misunderstood, but assistance could be sought from others, carers, the social worker or even the solicitor. And if the young person 'wanted it all over and done with', as some did, the leaflet could be ignored.

Of the four young people subject to applications for secure accomodation orders, two said that they could remember having received a leaflet, one of which was from the guardian. James found a leaflet left by the independent representative attached to the secure unit on his first night there. He had never been in a secure unit before, was locked in his room for the night and afraid. He was unable to sleep and read the leaflet because 'it was the only thing left to read.' The leaflet informed him about the unit and residents' rights, including the right to request a meal at any time if they had missed one. James who had missed a meal decided he could ask for something to eat. James remarked that he was pleased to have the leaflet. It helped to allay his fears about the unit and relieve his hunger. He kept the leaflet and referred to it during his stay.

None of the solicitors had leaflets for children and young people about their role and practice. The solicitors' practice of following the lead of the guardian and the lack of a common approach by the guardians on the panels studied would have made it impractical to do so except in the most general way. But this was probably not the reason for the lack of leaflets. The researchers were unaware of solicitors, other than the Official Solicitor, providing such leaflets. The Solicitors Family Law Association is considering producing a pack to be given to children about their rights when proceedings have ended and a care order has been made.

One type of written information sometimes given to children and young people was the contact address or telephone number for their guardian ad litem or solicitor. The guardians gave the researcher a variety of different ways young people could use to contact them. One guardian gave children and young people her personal mobile phone number, although she expressed some concern that one day this might be abused. Another 'employed' guardian said that she was happy for the young person to contact her at the guardian office. 'If I am not there then someone would pass on a message.' Two 'fee-attracting' (self-employed) guardians said that the young person should contact them through the solicitor's office. 'After all there would always be a secretary there to take a message.'

Three young people recalled having their guardian's telephone number written on a leaflet given to them by their guardian. However, it was not always clear how young people who were not given written information (letters or leaflets) would obtain this contact information. Some, but not all, of the solicitors wrote to their young clients, some letters just confirmed appointments but others gave a brief written account of information provided. All the solicitors' letters gave the contact number and address for the solicitor, making it possible for the young person to get in touch. Whether or not they wrote letters all the solicitors gave a contact number when they met their young clients, usually by handing them a business card.

There could be practical problems for young people trying to telephone representatives. Giving a telephone number to carers could not be assumed to make it possible for children or young people to telephone if they wanted to do so. Children may need to seek permission from carers or others about having access to, or using a telephone, particularly for expensive calls to mobile phones. As one solicitor noted:

> '[I don't often get calls from children] I suppose that is because some children may not necessarily have free access to a telephone. I wouldn't have let my children have free access to a telephone.'

Telephones could also be intimidating. One solicitor, recognising this, had reminded the secretary to take special care to put young clients through.

Very few children attempted to ring their representatives; with one exception, those who did so wanted to rearrange the times of appointments.

However, one child told his guardian, during a visit, that he had tried to ring him but he got the answer machine so put the phone down. His guardian explained that at times he was working and so could not answer the phone. There was no further discussion about the reasons for the telephone call.

Overall, young people said that they valued having written information and contact numbers. Tom told the researcher that the actual leaflet was not suitable to someone of his age but nevertheless he felt that it was important to have and keep. Another young person who had not made any telephone calls nevertheless said he was comforted by the fact he had a leaflet with contact information 'just in case'.

INFORMATION FOR CHILDREN AND YOUNG PEOPLE – A REVIEW OF LEAFLETS

Thinking about the written information provided to the children and young people in the study and their comments on it as well as those of the guardians ad litem prompted the researchers to look more widely at the leaflets devised by, and for use by, guardians ad litem. Through contacts with panel managers and individual guardians the researchers collected 25 different leaflets. Not all of these are still in use. In responding to the request to provide leaflets panel managers frequently commented that leaflets were being, or going to be, revised. The availability of leaflets is not synonymous with their use. No panel appeared to require the use of a leaflet; leaflets devised by one panel may be used by guardians on other panels. Some panels produced leaflets for parents, leaflets for other professionals, and two leaflets one aimed primarily at younger children and another, with more information (and often fewer pictures), at young people. Individual guardians selected whether to use a leaflet (Winn Oakley 1998, 32).

One striking thing about the leaflets was that a great deal of effort had been made to produce attractive leaflets as a way of communicating key points to children and young people. Although some leaflets used only black writing and line drawings on coloured paper, five of those collected had colour illustrations and text. In some cases the pictures had been drawn by children. Illustrations frequently included boys and girls and young people from different ethnic groups. Bright fashionable colours, orange, yellow, red and blue, were popular choices, particularly for leaflets produced for young children. Leaflets produced specifically for older children were colour coordinated with teenagers in mind. Black, purple and green were favoured for this age range, although black print on a purple background did not make for easy reading. And two leaflets, aimed primarily at younger children, had text that was far smaller than the print of an adult paperback.

Most of the leaflets included information in pictures and/or text; one included puzzles. This could be engaging and informative. For example, a word search could reinforce the recognition of a new term like *guardian ad litem*. The message of a dot-to-dot which revealed a dragon was more opaque (Figure 1).

There were wide variations in the amount of information contained, even taking account of the style and the use of illustrations to explain aspects of the process, as can be seen from the quotes below about going to court. This was the case even where leaflets were for the same age group.

Leaflets were clear, informative and concise, providing basic information in an attractive and digestible form. The contents tended to be focused on the role of the guardian; leaflets had been written by guardians. One leaflet made no mention of the solicitor. Most leaflets provided a space for the guardian to include their name and telephone number and in all but two cases, leaflets included spaces for the name and telephone number of the solicitor too. Those guardians who used leaflets confirmed that they would add this information to the leaflet before passing the leaflet on, but in interview some guardians said that they would leave the space for the solicitor's address and telephone number blank unless they were sure that the solicitor consented to this.

The leaflets indicated very different ways of explaining key aspects of the guardian's role or the court process, as can be seen from the following examples, which illustrate different answers to the question *who sees the guardian report?*

'Once your Guardian ad Litem has completed her/his enquiries, s/he will write a report for the court.'

'You will have a chance to see the report your Guardian ad Litem has written, as will your parents and your social worker.'

This is not merely a matter of style, these leaflets are describing different processes. The first implies that only the court, frequently used as a synonym for the judge or the magistrates, sees the report whilst the other reveals, as is the case, that the parties have access to it. Access to the report was a matter which confused some children and young people. Not all were aware that their parents saw copies of it. The second leaflet may also mislead; guardians in the study did not always show children their report, even where children expected this. Neither leaflet reflected the practice of most of the guardians in the study, which was to show the child or young person only a small part of the report which gave an account of their wishes and feelings.

Apparently quite subtle variations may give very different impressions to young people; for example, what can happen if the child or young person disagrees with their guardian ad litem (Figures 2 and 3).

Figure 1   Extract from the current Lincoln Panel of Guardians Ad Litem and Reporting Officers leaflet for children. Reprinted here with kind permission of Panel Manager, Roger Sharp, on behalf of copyright holder Lincolnshire County Council, Lincoln

Sometimes Guardians and Children do not agree about what is best. If we do not agree you can talk to your solicitor who will make sure the court knows what you want to happen.

Figure 2 Extract from the Birmingham Panel of Guardians Ad Litem and Reporting Officers current leaflet for children. Reprinted here with kind permission of Kate Griffiths on behalf of copyright holder Gill Jones, Panel Manager and Birmingham Social Services Department, Birmingham

The first (Figure 2) makes a specific reference to the child's right to speak to the solicitor and the solicitor's role in conveying the child's own views to the court, linking these to conflict with the guardian. The second (Figure 3) is less explicit, leaving it to the child to work out that he or she needs to speak to the solicitor. It also reflects that disagreement with the guardian is unusual, suggesting perhaps that the young person ought to agree with their guardian. However, the back of this leaflet (Figure 4) does list children's and young people's rights.

Figure 3 Extract from the IRCHIN leaflet for children. Reprinted here with the kind permission of Judith Timms, Chief Executive of the National Youth Advocacy Service (NYAS), 1 Downham Road South, Heswall, Wirral, Merseyside, L60 5RG. Please note that this leaflet is no longer current and will be replaced by a leaflet to be produced by NYAS. IRCHIN and ASC having combined to form NYAS at the end of 1997

> **'YOUR RIGHTS**
> - The court must consider *your* interests and welfare above everything else
> - The court must consider *your* wishes and feelings
> - The court must consider *your* needs
> - The court must consider special things about *you*, like your background and race
> - The court must consider *your* contact with *your* family, brothers and sisters
> - Your guardian ad litem (GAL) must safeguard *your* interests'

Figure 4

Differences in ideology are evident too. Whilst one leaflet may take a more paternalistic stance on some issues, others appear more child rights oriented, as for example, in these statements about young people attending the proceedings, taken from three different leaflets.

'Children don't usually go to Court themselves.'

'You may have to be there for some of the time, but not for very long.'

'They will also ask you if you want to go to Court to hear what is being said.'

Not only may these reflect the practices in the areas where they are used and the beliefs of the guardians who use them, they also convey a view to the young person about the part they play in the hearing. The first implies that it is unusual to go, or even to want to go, to court. It suggests that it is not worth asking if you can go. The second suggests a requirement to attend but only for a fleeting visit. The third suggests that attendance is a matter on which the young person can express an opinion and suggests, incorrectly (see Chapter 7), that this is a matter of their choice.

The Department of Health's leaflet for children and young people gives a more nuanced account of this issue:

'You may not have to go to court at all if you don't want to. The court can decide without your being there. But if you are old enough to understand what is happening you should think about whether you want to be there. This is something you can talk about with your solicitor and GAL. You may want to know exactly what is going on, or you may want to stay away altogether. You may choose to be in court some of the time; perhaps you will choose to come in at the end when a final decision is made. The court can also decide that you should not go to court if what is going to be said might upset you.

When you are old enough to understand what is involved you can tell the court that you want to be there for all or part of the hearing. The court will only go against your wishes if it thinks that it is very important to do so.' (DH 1991b, 12)

Even in an area which is less contentious, telling the child what the court has decided, quite different messages were given, as can be seen from two other leaflets.

In one, under a picture of the guardian waving from their car there is a caption:

'When the court decides what should happen in the future, my job ends. I will visit to explain what this means for you, and to say goodbye.'

In another the following text is printed:

'Who will tell me what the court decides?

One of the people who care for you will tell you. Perhaps your parents, your foster carers or your social worker. Perhaps your guardian ad litem or solicitor may tell you.'

The second leaflet may accurately represent the practice in the areas where it is used but actually provides very little real information. It does not state who will provide information, or when this will happen. The use of the words 'perhaps' and 'may' gives the impression the guardian does not know, and even that the young person might not find out at all.

CONCLUSION

In their interviews the children and young people generally remarked favourably on being given written information about the process. Although they sometimes reflected that they had not understood leaflets or letters, they liked having them and had kept them. Leaflets had given them information and had prompted some questions which might not otherwise have been asked. The guardian service as a whole needs to develop a policy on the provision of information for children and young people.

It is not enough to provide a leaflet. Written information must give a clear and accurate picture of the process to make it easier for children and young people who want to know more to know whom and what to ask. Information on tape should be made available, particularly for young people who have difficulty with reading. But whilst there are variations in the practices of guardians, solicitors and courts it is not possible to publish leaflets which are both simple and accurate. Standardisation of the court process is an essential part of ensuring good access to information about it. Guardians and solicitors need to adjust their practice to the needs of the individual child or young person but not to an extent which denies their rights or precludes an understanding of what is going on. The standardisation of practice would allow the production of a range of leaflets for use nationally with different age groups, ability levels and for different proceedings. The provision of leaflets for use across the country would help to give the service an identity. Good quality information for children and young people would also be useful in informing parents, carers, teachers and other professionals who only have limited involvement with the court proceedings, about the process that the children they care about are facing.

7

REPRESENTING CHILDREN AND YOUNG PEOPLE

'The purpose of the guardian's liaison and communication with the court is not to ease the passage of the case through the courts as an end in itself but to secure the welfare of the child by so doing.'
(DH 1992, 102)

THE CHILD AS CLIENT

Central to the discussion of representation are the issues of who represents whom and what is the purpose of representation. On the face of the documentation it appears that it is the child who is being represented. The child has party status, he or she is a respondent in the proceedings (FPR r. 4.7). The proceedings and the legal aid certificate are in the child's name. The guardian does not have status as a party. However, the court rules provide for the child's solicitor to be appointed *by* the guardian and require the solicitor to take instructions *from* the guardian except where the solicitor considers that the child wishes to give conflicting instructions and is competent to do so. Children are usually absent from the court; the guardian occupies their place in court.

Guardians emphasised both the child's particular circumstances and their own need for a solicitor they could trust as criteria for selecting solicitors but usually made appointments *before* they had met the child when they had only the briefest details about the case. Guardians referred to the solicitor as *my* solicitor whereas some solicitors stressed that *the child* was their client.

> 'It is one of the things you have to make clear time and time again to almost everybody in the case that you are the solicitor for the child. Even very experienced child care barristers make that mistake and refer to you as the solicitor for the guardian.'

> 'I work better [than barristers] because I know who I am representing. I have seen the child, even when you see a baby it makes a difference because you have this picture in your mind of who your client is.'

Being *the client* did not necessarily amount to very much.

'Some guardians just expect me to turn up at court and they will probably make an appointment to see me beforehand and brief me with what is going on. And obviously so long as I have satisfied myself in cases where I need to take instructions, then so long as I have seen the clients then that is OK.'

Most solicitors had only limited contact with the young person, seeing them only briefly and saying little to them. Most thought it was unnecessary for them to write to young people, either to explain what was happening, or the outcome of the case; discussion of the guardian's report was the guardian's task not theirs.

There were some solicitors who did not consider the child as the client.

'The guardian is the client and it is right that the guardian chooses the solicitor. The guardian will tell the solicitor what is wanted. As you build up it will be more of a joint partnership.'

And even if the child was the client the guardian was 'vicariously the client' and determined how the case was handled, not only because of giving the instructions but also because solicitors had to fit in with guardians to maintain their flow of work.

'You handle the case by the type of guardian you have got. The guardian affects the solicitor's role. I prefer to work with conscientious guardians who are not always clock watching and are mildly interventionist . . . You can't say boo to your guardian else you won't get any more work.'

The distinction between these approaches was sometimes obscured by references to the partnership between guardians and solicitors:

'The solicitor will cover the work in partnership with me.'

The guardian stands between the solicitor and the child. Children obtained their knowledge about the role of the solicitor from the guardian, solicitors relied on guardians for introductions to the child and information about the child.

'[The guardian ad litem] explains who everybody is . . . and they tend to know before I go.'

Some guardians expected solicitors to defer to them in order to determine whether and when they should see the child. Five of the 12 solicitors in the study only saw the child with the guardian and two, who had acted for the child previously, did not see the child at all during the course of these proceedings.

'No, solicitors do not go out to see the child by themselves. I always accompany them. The solicitors that I appoint will see all children, including babies . . . Solicitors await moves from the guardian.'

'I do find it's very difficult . . . because I find that solicitors still want to hear from the child themselves. So I do find I have to compromise with my own views with some solicitors. I've got one solicitor who will accept what I say . . . I've worked with her the most. But there are solicitors who actually want to hear it from the child.'

When solicitors saw children they were working for the guardian.

'If I am tied up in another case I expect the solicitor to see the child regularly when necessary. To keep the child informed for me.'

Case conferences and other social services meetings

While proceedings are pending the social services department may convene various meetings to plan or review the child's protection, or to consider plans for the child's future care. Different terms, case conference, review conference and planning meeting, are used for these meetings. They are likely to involve some staff from other agencies who work with the young person, for example health visitors, school nurses, teachers and police child protection officers as well as social workers. The emphasis on working in partnership has led to invitations being extended to parents.

The ambiguity of the solicitor's position was sharply demonstrated in their different attitudes to attending social services meetings about the child's care depending on whether they were acting for parents or for children. *Working Together* provides guidance on attendance at case conferences by guardians.

'Since their duty is to represent the interests of the child in court proceedings, it should be exceptional for GALs to take part in case conferences except in the case of a child protection conference following an application for an emergency protection order (EPO), or interim care order, when it might be helpful for them to be present as part of the process of gathering information for the court. The GAL would be present as an observer, not a participant, given his/her position as an officer of the court. (DH 1991a, para. 4.9)

According to the guardians the practice of inviting them to case meetings varied in the different local authorities where they worked. Most did not routinely attend when invited and would not stay if parents were asked to leave, as occurred in some authorities.

'When the parents left at half time for the decision-making to be done behind closed doors then we [guardian and solicitor] would always leave at the same time so that they could see we were not taking part in the final deciding.'

The guardians were most concerned to be seen as independent of the local authority and to avoid any confusion in the parents' minds that they were party to local authority decision-making.

'I go occasionally to case conferences. I would be very wary. I would not want to take part in case conferences as such.'

'I think one of my decisions as to whether I go would be whether the parents are going to be in attendance, if there is any confusion about what my role is in the parents' minds then I would not go because it is extremely important that independence is maintained.'

'Guardians cannot be seen to be proactive. They must be observers and be seen to maintain their independence.'

In recognising that planning for the child's future care is crucial, Law Society guidance states that it can be 'both helpful and important' for the child's solicitor, or a representative of the firm, to attend the child protection conference, either to accompany the child or attend on his or her behalf (Law Society 1994). The solicitors were not always invited to case conferences and some had experienced difficulties in obtaining payment from the Legal Aid Board for attending. Some expected to attend either with the guardian or alone, others considered that this was a task for the guardian and would only go if requested by the guardian. The guardian's attitude to attending case conferences determined whether some solicitors were invited or attended.

'I think they [social services department] get bogged down in seeing us as the guardian's solicitor rather than the child's, and guardians don't generally go to case conferences in this area . . . it's just a local practice, there's nothing to stop them but they don't tend to because I think they feel that that compromises their independence.'

There were advantages for the guardian of the solicitor attending; their notes were more detailed than the minutes and the solicitor could ask questions 'without being sucked into the social services department machine'.

However, solicitors who did attend case conferences were also concerned not to compromise the guardian's independence.

'You may be asked for an opinion but more it is like you are a watching brief at the case conference.'

'As I see it the role at that stage is an observer . . . Unless I thought that the children's views were being wrongly represented.'

This approach to case conferences was in marked contrast to that of the same solicitors when they were representing parents.

'I nearly always go to the case conference if I am acting for parents. Not so much so if I am acting for the child.'

'Some local authorities do not like or invite solicitors to case conferences. This is particularly so when you are representing the child. You may need to cajole them along once you have found out when the conference is. If I am acting for parents the exclusion is not so tight.'

'I like to go to case conferences and hear it . . . see who is involved. All the case conferences that I have been to I have been on behalf of parents.'

Advocacy at case conferences was part of representing inarticulate parents who were clients:

'I now attend cases conferences for parents . . . You may well need to advocate on their behalf. They may be parents who are unable to speak up for themselves, my presence may facilitate agreement between the parents and the local authority.'

One guardian felt that case conferences ought to provide guardians with an opportunity to share their perspective and influence decisions before the hearing:

'It can be difficult for a guardian to intervene sometimes in a conference and to share views. It is too late to raise issues afterwards. The vehicle to share views is not there.'

Case conferences are often forums for debates about the care plan for the child. Attendance by solicitors acting for the child may enable the solicitor to participate and place the child's wishes of where to live, whom to live with and what contact to have, firmly on the local authority's agenda, enabling them to be considered fully. Non-attendance may mean a loss of opportunities to get the best deal for the child client.

In the study, one guardian did not attend the local authority case meeting and was unaware of the local authority care plan for the child, which had been discussed there, until just before the final hearing. The plan conflicted with all the wishes of the child. The guardian raised her concerns while waiting for the hearing but was told that such issues should have been debated much earlier on. No mention was made of the reasons the solicitor did not attend the case meeting.

Preparing the case

Although solicitors may follow the lead of the guardian ad litem, their duty to receive documents on behalf of the child, their expertise in relation to drafting documentation for the court and their position as an advocate on the hearing give them a role in determining the part the child party plays in the preparation of the proceedings. Guidance from the Solicitors Family Law Association cautions solicitors against letting children become too involved (SFLA 1995, D3). The practice of children giving evidence in these cases is unusual and is viewed unfavourably by the High Court (*Re D.* 1997, Singer J.).

The young people in the sample cases had very little involvement in the preparation for the proceedings. Only one child was shown copies of statements filed in the proceedings. The solicitor decided that this child needed to see a parent's statement in order to be able to formulate opinions about the situation. In interview solicitors said that older children would be shown statements if they asked.

> 'I think a child of that age [15 years], if a child is saying, "I want a copy of that statement" . . . then I feel duty bound to give it to him.'

However, given the limited information young people had about the proceedings it was far from clear that they knew they could ask to see documents. What knowledge children had of the views of the other parties to the proceedings was generally filtered through the guardian or solicitor. However, children were not insulated from the facts, in most cases their experiences had led to the proceedings; they might also have received information about what was going on from social workers, carers or parents.

THE GUARDIAN'S REPORT

No statements were filed by any child or young person, although this might have happened had a young person been instructing the solicitor. In the sample cases the children's main communication to the court was through the guardian's report; only six children (four of whom were involved in secure accommodation proceedings) attended any of the hearings and even saw the judge or magistrates. However, guardians did recall rare cases where children had written to the judge or spoken to the judge in private.

When guardians had completed their report they sent it to the court. The Court Rules impose a duty on court staff to serve a copy on each of the parties; sending a document to the child's solicitor is the usual way of serving it on the child (FPR rr. 4.8(4)(a), 4.11(7)). Some guardians took responsibility, with the solicitor, for ensuring that the other parties received a copy, others left this to the court. A variety of issues determined which course was followed. Guardians and solicitors were sometimes concerned about the time (and the cost) of doing something that the court should do. But distributing reports themselves might be seen as speedier and more reliable. Local practice in different courts was also a factor.

Both guardians and solicitors noted that reports belonged to the court and were sensitive documents; care had to be taken in distributing them. Parents who were not represented were generally informed that they could see the report at the court but guardians would sometimes go through the report with them. The child's solicitor received a copy of the report for the child.

A guardian's introductions to the child usually involved telling them that their job included writing a report for the court. They explained that they had to tell the court what the child wanted and they would show them what they were telling the court.

'I usually explain to them right at the very beginning that I am only going to be involved in order to write a special report . . . and that once I have written that report and talked to them about it I won't be seeing them again . . . which is why I object very strongly to guardians building up a very strong relationship with the child . . . It horrified me at one training when a judge said that the only person that this child got on with was the guardian . . . I thought that was abusive . . . because that guardian had allowed the child to become dependent.'

Some guardians offered young people the opportunity to state their wishes in the report either by asking the child to write that part of the report or by copying down exactly what the child said. Not all the children were engaged by this exercise.

'I ask if they would like to write a bit . . . not many do, they are happy for me to write it.'

Prior to the final hearing the guardians generally visited the young person to go through the report. This might be a draft for the child to read and correct or a final version. Guardians were anxious that young people should not learn information for the first time from the report and were concerned not to upset the child with accounts of new, sensitive information about the family, unpleasant facts, or criticism of parents. The time-limited nature of their role meant that they were not available to counsel and support the child in dealing with this new knowledge. Consequently, they were reluctant to let children read the whole report for themselves although they sometimes allowed older children to do so, particularly if they thought that concealing information would cause more damage than allowing access to it.

'I have to advise them that there may be some parts in that report that they would not want to read. I first try to dissuade them from that. If they insist on reading it, then I have actually let them read it, and then we have talked about it . . . You are talking about balance here. If the child thinks, "Oh my God she's saying something about me I don't know", then the balance is that you are going to leave the child not trusting you for the sake of perhaps a few sentences that may be a bit hard to hear really. The reports are quite skilfully written . . .

the judge knows what you are saying but the young person would have to read between the lines to know.'

Most guardians were selective in the parts of the report they shared with young people, stressing that it depended on the child's understanding and that they tried to protect children. They either read sections out or showed children the relevant parts.

'There's a section in the report where I have to talk about the child's current situation, the child's wishes and feelings, and part of the report addresses the welfare checklist in relation to the plans for the child. We go through that. When stuff is on the computer you can just print off the pages which relate to them.'

'My heart sank a bit, because I think there were things in there that I felt would be quite hurtful. And I was trying to skip pages a bit, just to protect her feelings really.'

'I usually only go through the report according to their understanding . . . I might not get through it all because parts of it can be critical of parents.'

Occasionally the guardian did not think it was worthwhile discussing the report.

'I didn't with [child] simply because he would have said, "Yes, I know what you are going to say and No, I don't want to." (The child concerned commented that he had seen all the previous reports but not this one.)

It was not always possible to engage children:

'She just read it to me . . . I weren't listening. It was boring.'

The solicitors generally left discussing the report to the guardian. The report was the guardian's work, guardians were better able to explain it.

'The guardian generally does that . . . because it's a guardian's report. It's not for me to interpret what the guardian was saying.'

Solicitors were also concerned about imparting new or difficult information, even though they might feel that their young client needed to know to participate fully in the proceedings. They were aware of the guardian's reluctance to do this, but they felt it was not part of their role and knew they could not provide ongoing support. Solicitors generally thought that they did not have the skills necessary for communication of such sensitive matters. One solicitor faced the following dilemma. Her 14 year old client was the subject of care proceedings following allegations of sexual abuse of a neighbour's child by her parents. Neither the social worker nor the guardian had explained this background to the young person. The solicitor, having been unsuccessful in persuading them to do so, took it upon herself to tell her client because she believed this knowledge was crucial for the young person's understanding of the issues. She built up her relationship with her client through making further visits before telling her about the allegations. Although no formal complaint was made against the solicitor, she was criticised by the social services department for stepping outside what they considered to be her role.

However, without sight or explanation of what the guardian was saying, the young people cannot agree or disagree with the guardian. The solicitor cannot know whether one of the two criteria for separate representation of the child are met. Moreover, by this point in the proceedings half the solicitors had effectively disengaged from the young person. Where this had happened the solicitor would only be aware that the child objected to the report if the child was able to express this to the guardian and the information was passed on. In two of the cases the child disagreed with the guardian's recommendations; in neither case was the solicitor seen to respond to this.

A few of the solicitors discussed parts of the report with the young person; these might or might not be the same parts the guardian had shown to the child.

'I summarise it to them. Invariably the guardian would have gone through with them anyway, so I am probably skipping over it to a certain extent at that stage, making sure that important points as far as I am concerned are understood and agreed.'

It might not be until this point that it became clear that the child disagreed with the guardian's recommendation. If he or she did and was competent to give instructions the solicitor had to take further steps to ensure that the court was aware of this.

'It might be a situation where the child needed to file a witness statement . . . and in that case I would need to do some more work in detail, particularly if the child was disagreeing with some comments in the guardian's report, and it would be better to deal with that in a witness statement.'

All the guardians and the solicitors were clear that the child could not be allowed to have a copy of the report, because of its sensitive nature and the Court Rules. This view does not reflect the Court Rules, which make children parties to the proceedings, provide that the solicitor accepts service of documents 'on behalf of the child' and impose a duty on the solicitor to advise children who have 'sufficient understanding' of the contents of documents (FPR r. 4.12(2)).

Young people's perspectives on reports

Most of the children were interested in what the guardian was going to tell the court. Many children said that they wanted to be able to read the whole report, and they were not satisfied with having parts read to them.

> 'She told us that she'd definitely tell us and she would show us her report. First she only showed us the part mentioning us. I would have liked to have seen all of it.'

Some children felt that they had not been given the time or opportunity to consider the report properly.

> 'I haven't had a chance to read it, I read it at court . . . but you know what I mean.'

> 'I would have liked to read it . . . all of it, but [my guardian] had to go.'

Some children also wanted to have a copy to keep.

Interest in the report was not confined to the older children. The children did not comment on whether reading the report might have been upsetting, nor on the length of reports. It was the right to know and not have information concealed which was important.

> 'It involves us . . . and if it involves us then we've got a right to see it . . . to know the truth now rather than find out later.'

One young person suggested that it should be clear to the court that the child had seen and agreed with the report.

> 'There should be a page [in the report] written by me to say that I agree . . . or the solicitor should hand it in separately.'

Young people's limited access to the report and to legal representation after the report has been prepared operates to undermine their ability to understand what is proposed and the reasons for it. It also means that the court may not have its attention sufficiently drawn to the matters which children regard as important. Restricting children's access to the report may help the proceedings towards their planned outcome but conceals possible conflict between the guardian and the child. Where disagreements arise at this late stage only children with active solicitors or those who are confident enough to contact their solicitor directly may be properly heard. The current practice of concealing much of the report from most children was not acceptable to them.

Guardians take enormous care to collect relevant facts and opinions and to record them accurately. Children know that information has been collected and that other adults have access to it. Although guardians' reports cannot be regarded as 'the truth' about the child's situation they do contain detailed information which may help the child understand events that have shaped their lives. For some children, particularly those who are brought up in public care or who move from care to live with relatives, the guardian's report will contain detailed information which might later be unavailable elsewhere. Sharing this information with the child just before the hearing cannot meet their long-term need to understand the past. However, withholding the report means that young people are denied access to accounts which could assist their understanding.

CHILDREN AT COURT, YOUNG PEOPLE AT COURT

Prior to the Children Act 1989 two distinct approaches were applied to children's attendance at court. In the magistrates' court, children over the age of 5 years had to be brought before the court for care proceedings unless they were indisposed, or in the case of an interim order, legally represented (CYPA 1969, ss. 2(9),22(1)). In the county court and the High Court, children's attendance was generally considered inappropriate, except in adoption, where it remains compulsory (Masson and Morris 1992, 222). Requiring the child's attendance was generally considered not to be in children's interests. The form and the content of the proceedings were inappropriate for children; proceedings were not conducted so that children could participate. Also, children's daily lives might be disrupted by court hearings, especially if they had been placed at a distance from their home area (ABAFA 1979, 18).

The Children Act 1989 gave the court complete discretion over the child's attendance at court (s. 95). The rules provide that the proceedings may take place in the absence of a child who is represented by a solicitor or guardian ad litem if the court considers this to be in the interests of the child, and the solicitor, guardian and child (if competent) have had the opportunity to make representations to the court (FPR r. 4.16). The guardian ad litem has a specific duty to advise the court of the child's wishes about attending court (FPR r. 4.11(4)(b)).

Decisions in individual cases are made in a context where magistrates and judges, taking their lead from the High Court, generally consider that attendance is not in the child's interests.

'To sit for hours or even days listening to lawyers debating one's future is not an experience which should be wished on any child.' (*Re C.* 1993, Waite J.)

'The court must always bear in mind that attendance in court is likely to be harmful to the child.' (*Re W.* 1994, Ewbank J.)

The Children Act Advisory Committee gave guidance strongly discouraging children's attendance at court. Only where there is some clear benefit should the child attend. 'The very nature of the legal process is such that the child's attention may not be fully engaged and consequently he or she might derive little benefit from being present' (CAAC 1994, 45). The 'child's views can always be sufficiently ascertained by guardians or welfare officers or, exceptionally their solicitor'. The decision about attendance should be performed by the trial judge at a relatively early stage of the proceedings (CAAC 1995, 52). Despite the view of the Magistrates' Association that it could often be in the interests of a mature child to be present at the proceedings and that the guardian ad litem was best placed to advise the court, the Final Report of the Children Act Advisory Committee repeated its earlier views, emphasising that the child's attendance should be regarded as exceptional and that this applied equally to the family proceedings court. It also warned that practitioners should be aware of the law in this area so that children were not misled on whether they would be allowed to be present in court (CAAC 1997, 36).

Not all the concern is for the child's welfare. The *Guide for Guardians Ad Litem in public proceedings under the Children Act 1989* also refers to 'the impact the child's presence will have on the other parties and the court itself'. It stresses that judges are 'understandably opposed' to children's attendance and will require carefully reasoned argument in support of the child's attendance (DH 1995, 74). The earlier *Manual of Practice Guidance for Guardians Ad Litem and Reporting Officers* stated, 'direct involvement in the determination of the case can help enhance the child's sense of worth and of being believed, and provide reassurance that the adult world is taking their distress seriously' (DH 1992a, 52). These different views all reflect what adults think is good for children rather than how children feel about attending or being excluded from the proceedings.

The view that children should not be at court is reinforced in material written for children about care proceedings. Bracewell J.'s introduction to *Not Alone*, the Department of Health's information pack for children about care proceedings, explains that it is intended for children 'who will not be attending their care proceedings' (DH 1995a). In a Children's Society booklet, *Meeting Your Guardian Ad Litem* (Moore and Lane 1992), which explains care proceedings for children, the child is shown as a rabbit and the judge or magistrates as wise owls. The rabbit is absent from the illustration showing all the other animals at the court hearing – a point immediately noticed by Carol, whose guardian responded, 'the rabbit doesn't go to court'.

All the guardians in the study noted that the county court judges were opposed to children attending court hearings.

'Magistrates will be more sympathetic to attendance than what judges will be. The magistrates would be more persuaded by the guardian than perhaps the judges are. You see the judges will know the law and the rulings and who has made the rulings and the magistrates won't be conversant with that. They will rely on their training which will tell them to follow the lead of the guardian.'

'The judges don't like it. Not tidy and it's not. It all strikes me that there's still this attitude that its grown ups' business.'

Going to court

Going to court has three different meanings for guardians and solicitors representing young people: visiting an empty courtroom to see what it looks like, being in the court building during the proceedings and attending the hearing. The first poses only logistical problems, arranging a convenient time with the court and agreeing it with the child and carers. Such visits can be 'therapeutically advantageous', helping the child understand the process and prepare for the final hearing (DH 1995, 74). The Children Act Advisory Committee has endorsed the practice of taking children to visit empty court-rooms. In its view, 'This enables the child to have a better understanding of court process and the roles of the people who will be making decisions about his or her life. This practice is clearly in the child's interest' (CAAC 1997, 36).

Some guardians and solicitors offered to show children the court; indeed this was a common response if children asked about going to court. Only rarely was it a precursor to attending a hearing. One guardian explained her reason for using such visits:

'You want to make the case real for the teenager . . . so you have to bring the court setting to them . . . and you have got to involve them as much as you possibly can.'

Visits may be interesting but add to the child's confusion about the process. A solicitor who often arranged such visits commented:

'Children are more interested in seeing the cells.'

Some young people enjoyed this educational visit and others would have liked to have had the opportunity.

'I haven't been to court but I've seen one. I thought it would look like it's shown on *The Bill*.'

'I would have liked to see how [the court] looked.'

A visit may have helped them to understand what was happening and how things were decided but some visits were disappointing:

'It was busy so I did not get to sit in the judge's chair. Next time I will get to sit in the big chair.'

Children did not necessarily view the offer of a visit to an empty courtroom as a way of helping them to understand the proceedings.

'No. I told her . . . like she said, "Well, I could go and show you round." And I told her, "I am not really interested in the architecture of the building."'

If young people are to be in the court building during the proceedings, more complex arrangements are needed to ensure that there is someone to look after them and to ensure that there are no inappropriate meetings or scenes with family members.

'You've got the advocates dashing around and the guardian going into rooms and talking to people. So you've got to have someone that can be with them the whole time . . . And it can't be left to the guardian and advocates because they are far too busy.'

These arrangements are also needed if the child has been given permission to attend but decides to leave. Attendance at the hearing required the court's permission, which was not a routine matter, particularly for pre-teenage children. It would often be easier not to seek permission for the child's attendance.

Only five of the 20 young people in the study attended the final hearing. Four were young people for whom secure accommodation orders were being sought; guardians and solicitors assumed that young people should attend these proceedings. The other was a boy of 15 years who was the subject of care proceedings. Arrangements were made for a 10 year old to be in court although he finally chose not to go. A 14 year old attended a directions hearing where an unsuccessful application was made for permission to attend the final hearing; had permission been granted, a new hearing date would have been needed to fit in with the child's holiday.

Professionals' perspectives

The guardians were generally uneasy about children being at court. They were concerned about the effect on children and about deviating from judges' views:

'On the whole I'm not happy about children going to court.'

'I think the judges think it's all a bit much for the child, and in some ways I think it is.'

'Most of the time I would try to dissuade them because their image of court and what goes on is not reality. It's just boring sitting around and if it is a case that gets to be agreed nobody gets to say anything so you don't see what has gone on, the decision has been made.'

They were also concerned about children seeing 'distressed parents', hearing 'really horrendous evidential stuff' or the reasons for the decision which 'pull families down'.

However, most guardians ad litem noted individual cases where they supported the child's attendance because hearings could be pleasant.

'I am going to agree to [an 11 year old] coming to court because it is a nice happy one where foster carers are applying for a residence order which will discharge the care order and his mother is not going to attend.'

'I felt that it was good that he went to court for the discharge of the care order . . . But in a way, that's stage-managed because you know it's a nice occasion.'

Or because something positive might result.

'I knew that [her parents] would be there and there has been no contact whatsoever. And I thought, maybe, it might just promote a little contact.'

Most of the solicitors interviewed viewed children's attendance more positively. They favoured allowing children to be present in some cases, at least for part of the hearing.

'I worry about children in general hearing all that's going on. I sometimes think that it's actually beneficial. And I've been involved in discharge applications which were doomed to failure when they [social worker and guardian] had encouraged the child to go in and listen. Because then . . . they could take on board the reasons why they couldn't go home. And I think that's fine.'

Solicitors thought children should attend discharge applications which were likely to be successful.

'It is something of an achievement to end being in care, they have big parties . . . big sort of coming out parties. I frequently feel in those cases that the judge or the magistrates should give them a pat on the back. It is a significant occasion, almost like an adoption.'

The solicitors emphasised children's rights and the importance of the child being able to decide whether they wanted to be there, a view which does not fit with guidance from the Children Act Advisory Committee.

'I am concerned that children are excluded too much.'

'I feel that it's wrong to force them to go. I think it can be more damaging. It has to be their choice.'

'I have been through the procedure when children over 5 had to go . . . and now it has changed to the situation where quite often children want to go and aren't encouraged to go and I don't think either system has quite got it right.'

Although theoretically the child can be given the option by a court direction permitting attendance this was not the usual response from the courts in the study area. Only one solicitor thought that she would be able to get such a direction for a child client because the magistrates would trust her decision; other solicitors emphasised the reliance placed on the guardian's opinion and the generally negative attitude to children's attendance in the county court.

'I think judges in the county court are more reluctant to have children there . . . I don't know why. They're just so different compared to lay people. They just feel that, "Oh well it's our decision."'

The difficulty they might experience in obtaining a direction permitting attendance impacted on the way guardians and solicitors discussed attending the hearing with the child, as one guardian acknowledged:

'It's no good giving the young person the impression that it's going to be agreed. They must know that it may not be possible.'

Rather than ask children whether they wanted to attend, some solicitors left it to the children to make the request.

'They will have known about going to court, they will know through me what going to court is about, because I will explain what my job is. In terms of giving them the option to go, it is strange, it is a conversation which evolves rather than you saying, "You don't want to go to court do you?" Or, "You can go to court if you want."'

But it was not clear that young people understood that they were expected to take the initiative. Discussions about attendance were not always followed through, leaving children unclear why they had not gone to court.

'[The guardian] asked me if I wanted to go and listen to what was said and I said, 'Yes.' But I didn't go. I don't know why, I just didn't.'

Observations during the study of discussions about court attendance between children and their representatives often included reference to the *'boring'* nature of the proceedings. This appeared to have discouraged some children's interest in attending. It may also have given some children the impression that decisions about their lives were not matters of interest.

A child's request to attend was not taken by all solicitors as justifying an application for permission to attend. But children who gave 'good' reasons were not to be dismissed on the basis that proceedings might be upsetting.

> 'As long as I fully explored with them the reasons why they want to go and, if it seems to me to be a valid reason . . . I mean, different people have a different way of dealing with things . . . I felt that part of her way of dealing with this [abuse] was listening to what was going on in court.'

A solicitor would not make an application for the attendance of a child who wanted to go to court for 'the wrong' reasons, such as meeting a relative, although as the quotation above illustrates, guardians sometimes wanted the child to attend for this purpose.

> 'Had she shown that competence she'd have wanted to be there just to hear what was said.'

Solicitors, like guardians, were concerned about the nature and content of proceedings and their effect on young people. They also had concerns about the way proceedings were conducted.

> '[Some judges] haven't got the added compassion that I think you need for care proceedings.'

> 'I once did a discharge application, local authority, guardian ad litem, solicitor for both parents, and the child. And the entire application was done in complete silence. Nobody said a word.'

Directions precluding the child' attendance were frequently made early in the proceedings when the nature and duration of the final hearing could not be known. In fact there were no contested final hearings in any of the cases in the study and this was clear before the date of hearing in all but two of the cases. Had the courts been aware of the nature of the final hearing when they considered the child's attendance they might have viewed it more positively. Young people would also have been in a better position to make an informed decision about whether they wanted to attend had they known there was to be only a short uncontested hearing.

Young people's perspectives

The young people's views about going to court covered the whole spectrum from complete antipathy to having anything to do with the proceedings to anger that decisions might be made behind their backs. Children's views were not age dependent, both younger and older children had strong views in favour of or opposed to being in court.

There were a number of different reasons why children did not want to go to court. Some appeared to regard the proceedings as irrelevant to them, possibly because they would not change anything or possibly because they thought that there was nothing they could say or do which would change the way the system would operate. Even the children who had been in care for some time had little or no experience of attending case conferences or reviews and being involved in decisions about their own lives. As one child said in answer to the researcher's question about whether he had wanted to go to court:

'I can't go. It isn't about me.'

Some young people linked courts with being a criminal. This is hardly surprising given the confusion amongst adults, the fact that some of the literature for children includes illustrations of the family proceedings court with police officers in uniform and that their visits to courts included trips to the cells.

'It took me about two orders to think that I'm not a criminal, you know. I thought, "Oh God, I'm a criminal. Only criminals come to court."'

This confusion added to their stress and made some children unwilling to go to court.

'I was very bothered about going to [the criminal court]. I was sick, hospitalized the once, I was so stressed.'

Other children did not want to go because of general anxiety about their situation:

'I said I wouldn't like to go 'cause I didn't want to know what happened.'

Or because they were concerned about meeting someone they had no wish to see:

'No. Because we had to be there with our mum actually there and I didn't want that.'

Other children simply felt that court would be 'boring' – a view encouraged by both guardians and solicitors – or that they had better things to do.

'I did but then I changed my mind. I had something better to do at school . . . it was our activity day.'

One older child who recognised (rightly) that his wishes would be determinative of the proceedings thought that there was no need for any proceedings:

'I think going to court was a bit stupid . . . I can't see why. If they wanted to make it quick and short they just had to ask us . . . to put it in writing . . . no we didn't want [contact]. Take this to [applicant] and say, "They don't want to see you, continue if you like but you won't get to see them." The social worker could have dealt with it.'

Indeed, although this application could not have been prevented, the child's solicitor could have made an application for its dismissal at an earlier stage.

The young people who wanted to attend court also gave various different reasons for this. Some clearly wanted to see and hear what was being said:

'I stayed in [court]. Some of these people, if anyone's talking about them behind their back, they don't mind. I don't like it.'

For others hearing the decision when it was given was important:

'That was what I wanted to start with.'

'If a child says that they should like to go then all the adults should let them go . . . because they will hear [the decision].'

Some of these children also wanted to be able to speak to the judge.

'[The judge] would understand . . . because he has heard it from me. He will understand because that is what judges do.'

Others were content to be represented:

'When I go in there I don't actually say anything. I just get [my solicitor] to say it all for me. I don't mind provided I'm in there . . . She will say whatever I want . . . I get too nervous.'

There were young people who wanted to go to court because they thought they would be able to see parents who were not being allowed contact:

'I would see where the judge sits and where my dad sits . . . I wish I went to the hearing.'

A court hearing also provided a day out from secure accommodation.

'Sometimes you have a lot of waiting around and sometimes you don't. I don't care if I have to be there six hours 'cos I get out of here [secure unit].'

The outcome

Most of the children and young people were not in court to hear what had been decided so other steps had to be taken to ensure that they knew and understood the outcome of the proceedings. Who told the child, how and when this was done appeared to vary from case to case. Young people were not necessarily told when or how they would hear. Lucy, who was interviewed for the research on the day of the hearing, was preoccupied with whether a decision had been made and unsure when she would know. It appeared that some professionals had lost sight of the importance and urgency that a court decision, even one confirming an agreed arrangement, could have for the child concerned. Arrangements to inform children of the decision were haphazard. Some children were phoned or sent letters by their guardian ad litem, others heard from carers who had been present or from their social worker.

'It was carer who told me. [my social worker] never tells me what goes on does she? . . . It was like they were relying on [my carer]. I don't really bother but my solicitor and guardian ad litem should have.'

Although most guardians and some solicitors made *goodbye visits* these did not necessarily satisfy the child's need to know quickly what had happened in court.

Should children/young people attend?

Clearly there can be no one answer to the question, *Should the child attend the court?* But there is universal agreement amongst professionals and children that children should not be required to attend. Views about court being damaging to children appear to be based on instances of long contested hearings which occur regularly in the High Court but are infrequent elsewhere. Guardians and solicitors see advantages for children in attending applications for discharge of care orders and care cases where residence orders are made. The control the court currently exercises over attendance of the child makes it more difficult for guardians and solicitors to engage with children over this decision. Young people's exclusion from the proceedings may contribute to their disengagement from the process. Better decisions might be made about the child's attendance (either by the court or by the child concerned) if the nature and length of the hearing were known at the time the decision was made.

CONCLUSION

Party status appeared to have little impact on the way the children and young people in the study were represented, and on the part they were allowed to play in the proceedings. The practices of the solicitors and the guardians inevitably lead to the question, *What benefit was there in the child having automatic party status in these proceedings?* In considering this question, it should also be noted that the children in the study were older than most children involved in these proceedings. Although the child was generally considered by both guardians ad litem and solicitors to be *the client*, there was little in the way the children were treated that made this apparent. Both guardians and solicitors shielded children from the process and tended not to encourage their active participation.

Party status usually brings with it the right to participate fully in the proceedings, to direct the way one's case is presented, to make applications, to see and respond to evidence and reports, to attend hearings and to decide whether to appeal adverse decisions. Although the guardian ad litem does not have party status, he or she has the power to make applications, call evidence and to seek to appeal. Without the guardian's involvement the court would not be able to have an adequate picture of the child's interests. Guardians ad litem can do these things because they stand in the place of the child in the litigation and instruct the child's solicitor. The child's party status shapes the court process even though it may not give the child active participation in it. Through the involvement of the guardian ad litem it enables the court to have a more complete picture and more active presentation of the child's interests than would be possible if the court only had access to reports from a court welfare officer.

An approach whereby the guardian ad litem takes over the case of the child or young person does not necessarily meet the needs of older, competent young people, who may wish to participate in the proceedings. But to require all children and young people to participate would be oppressive, particularly because parents can decide about their own active participation in care proceedings. If young people's knowledge of proceedings and opportunities to participate in them is to be facilitated, both the proceedings and representation need to be restructured to allow this to happen. This involves making a reality of the young person's party status by strengthening their relationship with their legal representative and reducing the court's discretion over attendance at hearings. As active parties young people should have sufficient information to be able to make informed choices about their involvement, for example whether they wish to make applications for contact or to attend hearings.

8

CHILDREN'S AND YOUNG PEOPLE'S AGENDAS REVISITED

There is a mismatch between the child's agenda and the power of the court. Many of the issues which most concerned the young people related to their day-to-day care, particularly where they would live and who would look after them, but these were matters for the local authority not the court. Guardians could have some impact on these matters by encouraging the social worker to look at particular issues.

Both guardians ad litem and solicitors agreed that it was legitimate for the guardian to contact the social worker from time to time during the course of the investigation; these calls could be used to remind or chivvy the social worker.

> 'And it is her job [guardian] to say to social services, "Have you done this? Have you done that."'

> 'It is often a matter of the practice is a bit lax or something and you just remind them about it and they will do it.'

Guardians were aware that work might not be done for the children despite willingness because the social worker lacked support with the authority to prioritise it. Whether or not this was the case, raising issues with the social worker might not have the desired effect. Guardians felt inadequate if children desperately wanted changes which they had not been able to achieve and were concerned that they had let the children down.

> 'All I would be able to do is go back to the social worker and say, "I'm not happy about this." And I have done that on occasions. I mean that's the hard bit of the job because I have had occasions when children have cried . . . they really cried and said they hated it. And you know, they expect that you . . . you know, you're their guardian, "Why can't you do something about it?" . . . And you feel you ought to be able to.'

Guardians viewed negotiation as a better way forward, it could achieve as good an outcome and leave the guardian with more positive relationships with social workers.

> 'I'm a great one for conciliation as well as trying to sort of work out . . . Now I'm not sure whether this is down to me and my skills as a guardian but I think it is probably more to do with coincidence. I don't have many contested, long drawn out hearings. And I do try and get negotiation. I think that is part of my role. Because you are never ever going to get ideal solutions in these situations. But if you can negotiate . . . I know the last year in a couple of cases, social workers said to me, "Well thanks, I really valued your contribution . . . and with your intervention I have been able look at situations a bit differently."'

The loss of contact with friends and family which many children experienced after coming into care was very important to them. This contact was not the focus of the proceedings because it was not in dispute: there were no applications relating to it before the court, the friends and relatives were not parties. It was just another responsibility of the local authority which could feature in the care plan but over which the court, the solicitor and the guardian had no control. The overriding concern was whether or not there should be an order. This was the context in which the guardians and solicitors were representing the children. This focus was also the deciding factor as to whether the solicitors accepted instruction from the child as opposed to the guardian. As long as the guardian and the child were in agreement about the making of an order, then any other areas of dispute did not necessitate separate representation. There were no cases of separate representation in the study. One solicitor referred to this issue in a past case:

> 'I have had one . . . she was clearly competent and I thought at one stage we were going to have quite a bit of difference between what the guardian was saying and what she was saying. But I don't think it was . . . There were certain things she wanted to be said. And at the end of the day she wasn't disputing the guardian's final conclusion [recommending a care order]. And we managed to get round it, "Well, although you're not happy with how she's reached those conclusions, you agree at the end of the day. You've still got the guardian. But I will tell the court you don't agree with this, you don't agree with that, but you are happy an order should be made." That's the thing to find out. What is the child's objection? Is it actually against an order?'

Solicitors and guardians wanted to try to achieve the best possible outcome for the child and recognised that many of the children had no one else who would support them but they were constrained by the limitation of the court's powers vis-à-vis the local authority. The court could refuse to make a final order but could not require the local authority to amend its care plan. Changes to the arrangements for the child's care could not be imposed by the court, as a guardian explained:

'I think it can be a problem but at the end of the day all you can do is point out the worries you've got about the care plan, you can't impose your own care plan on the local authority. . . . And I think the difficulty is that sometimes you are faced with a situation where you feel the care order is an absolute necessity for the child, but you don't like the care plan. But what can you do? Because the alternative is to put the child in a situation which probably would be too great a risk. What annoys me more is that I agree with the care plan and then twelve months on they've still not implemented it.'

Guardians had to accept their powerlessness or find other ways of achieving an improvement in the child's situation. The guardian's duty to carry out an investigation justified certain activity, such as contacting the extended family, which the local authority might not have undertaken.

YOUNG PEOPLE WHOSE AGENDAS WERE MET

Carol's solicitor took her into the empty court to familiarise her with the court setting. Subsequently, Carol, 14, who had learning difficulties, attended a directions hearing at the local magistrates court with her solicitor and guardian. The researcher was also present. Carol's solicitor put forward her request to attend the final hearing. Prior to this hearing Carol was excited and pleased to be at court. She understood that the magistrates would decide about her attendance at the final hearing.

At the directions appointment Carol sat between her solicitor and guardian. The local authority solicitor was present and so was the solicitor acting for her parents, who did not themselves attend. The court clerk told everyone to rise and the magistrates came into court. The solicitor for Carol reminded the court of the purpose of the hearing and put forward Carol's request. She explained that if Carol was to attend the final hearing then a new date would be needed as Carol was going away on holiday. The solicitor then explained that Carol's guardian was not in favour of Carol attending the hearing. The local authority solicitor also stated his opposition to Carol's attendance, as did the solicitor acting for Carol's parents, adding that his clients were continuing to oppose the making of a care order.

The magistrate smiled at Carol and spoke directly to her. Carol smiled back. The magistrate explained that she did not think that it was appropriate for Carol to attend the final hearing but thanked her for attending the directions hearing. She told Carol to go off and enjoy her holiday.

During the interview, the researcher asked Carol how she had felt about being at court and how she felt her request to attend had been received. Carol said that she was pleased that she had gone and that the magistrates had listened to what she had wanted. She had accepted their decision. She did not feel upset by their refusal.

Carol's parents withdrew their opposition and a care order was made in relation to Carol by agreement. The care plan for Carol was unchanged. She was to stay with her present foster carers and to have ongoing contact with her mother and father. Carol was pleased with the outcome of the proceedings.

Carol's solicitor referred to her request to attend the final hearing. She felt that Carol had been content with the magistrate's decision although the solicitor was uneasy that she had not made out a stronger case for Carol. She did feel her attendance at the directions hearing had served a purpose. She explained:

'Yes she wanted to go to court and meet everyone involved and it was sort of a compromise wasn't it?'

Lucy was the only child to be interviewed on the day of the final hearing at court. The court was considering the discharge of her care order in favour of a residence order to her aunt. The researcher arranged the interview for this day because there was the possibility that Lucy would leave her foster carer's home immediately the residence order was made. Given the timing of the research interview, Lucy's overriding concern was to know whether the order had been made so that she could go and live with her aunt. She constantly asked the researcher about the time and as to whether the court would have now considered the making of the order.

Lucy stated that she wished she had attended the hearing. She did not think that she had been given the option to be at court. She had not seen her solicitor throughout the duration of the discharge proceedings but did not think that that was a problem as she had got on well with her guardian. She did feel that the best thing would have been for her to be there at court and to tell the judge in person that she wanted to live with her aunt.

Lucy's care order was discharged and a residence order made in favour of her aunt. She left her foster home and went to live with the aunt.

Andrew, 15, was made the subject of an agreed care order. The local authority had been reluctant to apply to take out a care order on someone of Andrew's age but Andrew wanted to have the security of a care order so that he could continue to live with his aunt. She in turn needed financial assistance from the local authority in order to be able to care for Andrew. To facilitate this, she and her husband were accepted as long-term local authority foster carers for Andrew. Andrew was content with the outcome of the proceedings.

Sonia attended both her secure accommodation hearing and the care hearing concerned with her baby daughter. As a minor, the subject of secure accommodation proceedings, Sonia was entitled to the services of both a solicitor and a panel guardian ad litem. As a mother of a child who was the subject of care proceedings, Sonia was entitled to only a solicitor and not a panel guardian ad litem. This was so even though Sonia was still a minor.

Both Sonia and her solicitor recognised that she needed expert help in the care proceedings. As mentioned in the earlier chapter, Sonia's agenda had been to prevent her child from being in the care of the local authority but that her feelings of desperation had led to her absconding at court from the secure accommodation hearing. Sonia trusted her guardian ad litem who had encouraged her to give herself up. Sonia instructed her solicitor to make an application to the court for her guardian to be appointed to represent her in the care proceedings. Her solicitor sought the local authority's consent to this and the appointment was made. Sonia's guardian and solicitor succeeded in opposing the making of a secure accommodation order in favour of a supervision order, and succeeded in persuading the local authority to agree to Sonia's mother having a residence order for her child. Sonia now lives with foster carers but has contact with her child. She is working to ensure that she stays out of trouble and that eventually she will be allowed to care for her baby. Sonia stated:

> 'Having a guardian was a positive experience. If I didn't have a guardian and a solicitor I would have just given up on everything 'cause I felt I was not going to get her back.'

Alex was made the subject of an agreed care order with a view to his living at his aunt's home. She became a long-term local authority foster carer for Alex. Alex was pleased about this. Conditions in Alex's aunt's home were poor. She was a single parent, reliant on benefit and looking after five children under 10. Her home, on a run down estate, was overcrowded and in a very poor state. She was awaiting rehousing. At the end of Alex's interview, she asked if the researcher could help her as she desperately wanted the children to have a holiday. Clearly she needed considerable financial support for her family.

William's case is listed here as being a case that was finalised having met the young person's agenda. What is interesting about the case is the route William's representatives took to ensure that funding was available to support his care plan. William was not opposing the current application for a secure accommodation order but was going to oppose the next application as he was bored in the unit. A number of secure units are holding units only and as such do not attempt to address the young person's behaviour. The unit where William was placed was not simply a holding unit but had staff with therapeutic specialisms who could work with the young residents in trying to deal with their problems. This input may also address William's boredom in the unit. In order to be placed in this facility William had to be subject to a care order. To receive therapy he needed a funded care plan. His representatives had succeeded in getting the local authority to seek a care order for William.

His guardian explained:

> 'And he was beyond parental control. We felt that [William's] offences were very serious. And he is . . . at the age of 14 . . . to be a schedule 1 offender . . . there's no way back . . . And given that he needed specialized therapeutic input . . . One of the conditions of residence at [the unit] is that children are on a care order.'

By the time of the final hearing, there was still no funding available for the care plan. William's representatives knew that a care order on its own was insufficient for William's needs since lack of funding would mean the failure to implement the care plan. He needed therapy to address his behaviour as a schedule 1 offender. His representatives decided to hold up the making of the final orders until the local authority could confirm that funding was available for the care plan.

Both the guardian and solicitor feared for the safety of William and for the safety of other children generally, if William did not receive this input. The guardian explained her resolve to ensure that William had a funded and hence workable care plan.

> 'I think the thing that is possibly achieved is keeping on the local authority's back. They expect us to rubber stamp everything. And you never agree to do that. We kept hanging on with the interim orders when they wanted final orders. And to force them into decisions about funding. I mean the classic was that we had care proceedings which were fixed for a certain date . . . let's say it was the 10th December. But the decision about the funding was due to take place . . . on the 20th December. So they expected us to ratify a six month secure order and a final order without any guarantees that the care plan they had written for the court was capable of implementation. And they kept doing that throughout. On the whole, I'm not prepared to give the local authority carte blanche to have a care order when there is no clear care plan because I am not sure what the advantage to the child is.'

The guardian made the point that ill defined care plans were not in the young person's best interests. She insisted on there being a clear care plan for William before final orders were made at court. As a result of this action by William's guardian and solicitor, the local authority were forced into ensuring that funding was available for William's care plan whilst the court retained control of the case. Only then did the guardian and solicitor agree to the final hearing taking place when a secure accommodation order and care order was made by the court. William remains at the unit and is in receipt of therapy.

YOUNG PEOPLE WHOSE AGENDAS WERE MET IN PART OR NOT AT ALL

There were five cases, affecting eight young people, where significant issues remained outstanding even though the final orders had been made and the court's role had ended.

Peter, Sylvia and Martin were each to remain in local authority care under care orders but did not know who was going to care for them. Each of the care orders had been made by agreement. Each of the care plans referred to the children moving from their present foster carers to new long-term foster carers. New carers had still to be identified for each child. All three children referred to their concerns about not knowing who was going to care for them. For Peter this was particularly worrying because he was settled with his present foster carers and wanted to stay where he was.

The care plan for Peter was to move him from his present foster placement to another one out of the area. This would be Peter's third move since the proceedings had been started. It meant that Peter would not have any of his wishes: to stay in his home area, to remain with his present foster carers, or to remain at his present school. Peter's guardian told the researcher that she had been unaware of the local authority's plan to move Peter. She had not attended the local authority's case conference where the care plan was discussed. She thought it might even have taken place prior to her appointment. She was aware of the strong relationship that Peter had with his carers and his wish to remain at the same school. Peter's guardian met the social worker at court just before the final hearing. She asked why Peter had to move. Neither the guardian nor Peter's solicitor was given any reason for this. Both representatives later told the researcher that they had been unhappy with the care plan but felt unable to delay the making of the care order, which was uncontested.

Unlike William's guardian, Peter's guardian decided not to hold up the making of the care order although she was unhappy with the care plan. She did, however, get Peter's solicitor to raise her concerns with the magistrates in the hope that they would put weight behind the guardian.

> '[The magistrates] were told of [the issue] when we came into court . . . and they said that they hoped the local authority would not be unduly influenced by [the view the guardian disagreed with].'

Guardians' high status in the court meant that they got support from the court. It was less clear that homilies from the chair of the family panel or the county court judge had any impact on the local authority.

The lack of a clear mandate for addressing issues outside the control of the court, the limited and uncertain impact that these various strategies might have and pressures to avoid delay and focus on the proceedings discouraged many guardians from being very proactive.

Peter's guardian was unclear about the reason for the proposed move. It could have related to the perceived unsuitability of the current carers for Peter, the local authority's decision to respond to the mother's declared wish to avoid Peter, or a need to make the best use of scarce fostering resources. A more thorough investigation of the care plan might have indicated the local authority's reasons. Had this been a private law dispute the approach of the court would almost certainly have been to favour Peter's remaining with his current carers, where he was settled, over a move which would have disrupted his schooling and restricted contact. However, it is unclear that the court in care proceedings could legitimately have refused to make a final order even if the local authority's decision had been based on either of the first two possible reasons. The substance of the local authority's plan – a permanent foster placement and limited contact with parents – was not in issue, nor was the making of a care order. And there was no possible further assessment which might have identified another course of action. Even if the alternative foster carers had been identified so that the court could form an independent view on which placement was most suitable for Peter, it would have had no power to order where he was placed. That being the case, it is, perhaps, understandable for the guardian to decide not to investigate the local authority's reasoning and not to challenge the plan on the basis that it failed to take sufficient account of either Peter's wishes or his needs.

The care order was made. Peter would remain in his present placement until the local authority had identified a new one for him.

Peter did not attend the court hearing. His guardian visited him afterwards and told him of the local authority plans. His solicitor also planned to visit but was unable to do so because of other work commitments. Peter's solicitor wrote him a letter explaining the outcome of his case. Peter showed the letter to the researcher. It read:

'. . . [social worker] feels it would be better for you to move to another foster home outside [area] where you can stay while still continuing to see your dad regularly and your mum occasionally. This would mean you changing schools. So you talk to your social worker about that if you are not sure. I know you have told me that you want to stay where you are. [Social worker] hopes it can be arranged in time for you to start a new school after the summer holidays. The magistrates told your social worker that they were unhappy at the thought of you having to move. [Social worker] told [guardian] and myself that when a new home was found for you, you would be able to go and look at it and decide if you want to move there. So you have got a say in it. Everybody is trying their very best to help you. Different people sometimes have different ideas. So it is important that you let people know how you feel and what you want. Your wishes and feelings are important.'

The solicitor explained that Peter had a right to say what he thought about the new placement. He had a choice. He also reminded Peter to tell people about his wishes and feelings. Peter had already done just that for the court hearing. Peter said that he did not really understand all of the letter even though his foster mother had read it to him.

Peter's solicitor explained to the researcher why he had written to Peter.

'Yes he did like it at that house. I mean the main issue in that case was the care plan rather than whether there should be a care order . . . The cynic could say no we did not do any good because in the end the local authority conceived its care plan which [guardian] and I didn't agree with and we said that to the court. Ultimately the care order was still the right order and once a care order is made the case law is, as far as the court is concerned you have a choice, you can either make a care order and disagree with the care plan but know it is going to happen or make a supervision order but then you might not be protecting the child. So, in the end the care order was right, and I did try and persuade the local authority afterwards that their care plan was not right for Peter. At the same time I did not want to give Peter the thought that he could in some way undermine the care plan by misbehaviour because that wouldn't be in his interests either.'

It would appear that Peter's representatives had placed resolution of the outstanding issues firmly back on to Peter's shoulders. Now that the care order had been made he was unrepresented.

Sylvia accepted that a care order had been made at the final hearing at court and that she would move to live with long-term foster carers when they had been identified. In the meantime her social worker had told her that she would continue to reside at her present short-term foster home. Sylvia hoped that she would move soon. Sylvia said that her guardian had explained the decisions made at court. A care order had been made and there was to be no contact with her father. She stated:

'[the guardian] wrote me a letter telling me that a decision had been made and that I can't see my dad until I am 18.'

Sylvia said that she was not angry with the decision. Sylvia did not know her father's address (it had been deleted from the report she had seen) but she was aware that her guardian had visited him. At the end of the research interview Sylvia wrote a message for the researcher to pass on to Sylvia's guardian. It read:

'Tell her that when she goes to see my dad that I miss him and I love him. I hope to see him soon and give him lots of kisses for me.'

Sylvia's agenda at the end of the proceedings appeared to remain the same as her agenda during the proceedings. She wanted to move from her present placement and she wanted to have contact with her father. She had achieved neither of these.

Martin's solicitor and guardian both came together to visit him at his residential special school. Martin did not attend court. The proceedings lasted just over 12 months and at the final hearing a care order was made by agreement of the parties. There was to be no contact by Martin's father. He had withdrawn his application for a contact order having received an unfavourable assessment. Martin's solicitor and guardian visited Martin together at his residential special school to explain the outcome of the proceedings. The researcher accompanied them.

Martin's guardian told him about the care order and that he would remain in local authority care until he was 18. He also told Martin about his father's assessment and how the court had concerns about Martin seeing his father. Martin's solicitor then talked to Martin about the court's decisions. She told Martin that he was not to see his father and asked him if he understood. Martin said that he did. A little later on Martin asked his solicitor for his father's telephone number so that he could ring him. Martin's solicitor then had to explain to Martin that he was not to have any contact with his father. Not to see him nor to speak to him on the telephone.

Martin's solicitor later explained to the researcher that Martin had been having telephone contact with his father for some time but that this was stopped when the care proceedings had begun. Clearly Martin had understood that telephone calls would be permissible.

Martin asked his representatives about having contact with his cousin. This had been part of his agenda during the proceedings. His guardian told Martin that he was aware of Martin's wish to see his cousin and that he had told the social worker about this. The guardian said that he was sorry that nothing had been arranged. Martin asked his representatives about the name of his new foster carers. This matter was also of great concern to Martin. Martin's solicitor again apologised to Martin because this had not been sorted out.

Later the guardian commented upon social services failure to arrange contact with the cousin.

'There were some members of his family who might have been interested in having some contact with him. They will say quite clearly that they wanted someone from social services to contact them . . . Often I find . . . the local authority will not contact extended family and they appear to have two kinds of reasoning for this. One is, "If the extended family were interested in this child, they will contact us." And that does not take into account that many people don't have contact with, or experience of, social services and many people feel that, "If our views counted, if we had rights or something, somebody would contact us and ask us." Another reason is occasionally that they [social services department] look at a child, and they think, "Well this is how the parents have turned out, the grandparents and the aunts and uncles can't be much better." And I think there is a third reason in there, the lack of time.'

Martin asked his representatives about his weekend foster placement and whether this had been sorted out for him. Martin had asked about this issue during the proceedings. Both representatives apologised to Martin because this had not been sorted out. They both told him that the social services should be dealing with it. Martin's solicitor said that she would write to the social services about this matter and ask them what was happening. She promised to let Martin know about this.

Martin was having regular contact with his sister, who was already living with long-term foster carers under a care order. Social services arranged for her to come and visit Martin at his school. He was also having some contact with his mother. His new baby half sister was now the subject of care proceedings. Martin's guardian told the researcher that the judge was disappointed that another guardian was acting in this matter. (Martin's guardian was no longer a member of the appropriate panel although arrangements could have been made for his appointment.) The judge was concerned that there were a number of matters still outstanding. Had the guardian acted in both proceedings then perhaps Martin's outstanding issues could have been kept 'live' in the court. As it was no one was now looking out for Martin.

At a later interview the solicitor gave the researcher an update of the situation. She had closed Martin's care file but had opened a new file for Martin headed 'accommodation' and had, as promised, written to the social worker about the need for Martin to be allocated a new foster carer. She had yet to receive a reply. She was not going to be paid for this work and was not sure whether she should be doing it. She would write to Martin because she had promised to do this. She was frustrated about what could be done if social services did not sort the matter out. She was aware that Martin would be justified in bringing a complaint against social services but asked who would complain for Martin; she had no authority to act and Martin, because of his learning difficulties, would need adult help to take the matter further. She commented:

> 'I said I would do that . . . I wanted to make it clear that I was just passing on the information and that that was all. I am not sure it is the right way forward . . . So that is what I have done, rightly or wrongly and I did agonise about whether it was wrong. It's really, perhaps a gentle way of asking. Social services know that I want to know. But if I do not get a response soon then I suppose I have to write to Martin and say, "You do have this option if you want to take it up." . . . but I don't know how you would handle it . . . Well I promised I would write it. . . . Oh I wouldn't be handling it. No it wouldn't be me that would be doing it and I don't know how he would handle it given his difficulties . . . he is left with, he has absolutely no one . . . I am not sure that I should be sorting that out afterwards but I have done it and I am going to do it. I don't get paid for that but that is not the point.'

Martin's guardian also commented about his frustrations that matters remained outstanding after proceedings had ended. He did not have faith in the complaints procedure but there were other issues too.

'I am normally not keen on making complaints . . . But the other thing is that if you make a formal complaint you can put people's backs up and you have to have a working relationship with these people in the future so it is not the best way of going about things.'

For both Sylvia and Martin there were concerns about contact with a paedophile father. Both young people were told that the court had said that they could not have contact with their fathers until they were 18 years old. From the court's position this is the only power it has, restrictions of contact made in care proceedings cannot go into adulthood. In terms of Sylvia's and Martin's welfare this seemed an inadequate response which may have left them more vulnerable. The danger their fathers posed would not end when they grew up; they and any children they might have are likely to continue to be vulnerable. Formally terminating contact when they were very isolated did nothing to reduce their longing for their fathers. It was not clear that any of the professionals had tried to explain these issues to Sylvia and Martin. Indeed, Martin, who had been abused in care, had still not received sex education or help with self-protection which had been recommended in an earlier assessment.

Like Peter, Sylvia and Martin, Edward was now the subject of a care order by agreement. However, the care plan for Edward was for him to move to live with his aunt, who lived some miles away in another county. Edward was keen to move to his aunt's but there was no immediate plan for this to take place. This was unfortunate because Edward hated having to stay at school at night. If he moved to his aunt's home, he would attend a day school. Edward had continued to ask his guardian and his solicitor if he could return to his foster carer's home at night.

Edward was also concerned to maintain contact with his family. He had only seen his mother once, recently on a visit to his school, and he still lacked contact with his siblings and stepfather. The guardian had debated the wording of the care plan at court. Taking a more proactive stance could bring the guardian into open conflict with social services and make the proceedings unacceptably adversarial. Nevertheless she took this approach in relation to contact.

'Mother did not contest the care order and was not present at the final hearing. I took exception to the wording in the care plan about her contact. I felt that it should be more proactive on the social services side, that they should endeavour to make contact with mother to try and set up some contact with Edward. I think the local authority saw me as interfering in this matter. I wanted the words to reflect social services trying to make contact happen. Not leave it to mother to contact social services. She wouldn't have done that.'

The solicitor noted that the local authority had reacted badly at the hearing.

'Yes, I think, I certainly hoped at the final hearing when I ended up liaising between the guardian and [the barrister] and social worker and the strange solicitor from the local authority and they started to seriously argue about contact and it all got completely out of hand . . .'

The guardian and solicitor were both in favour of the care order being made but were unhappy with the local authority's inactivity. They had complained to the local authority about what they perceived to be unnecessary delay in implementing the plan prior to the final order being made at court. Edward had had little contact with his aunt who was intended to be his foster carer. Neither the guardian nor the solicitor was optimistic about the progress of the plan once proceedings were at an end. Edward's solicitor commented:

'The other issue was that they [social services] were dragging their heels with placing [Edward] with his aunt . . . an argument did start about dragging their heels and not being prepared to place him until police checks had been done. I think by being on the ball as we were, we did get Edward down to [place] where he should have been. He only went down there twice, which was disgusting in my view.'

After the conclusion of the proceedings the guardian enlisted the help of the local Children's Rights Officer to monitor Edward's move, in the hope that such involvement would effect it as quickly as possible. The guardian and solicitor delayed their usual goodbye visit to Edward because they had hoped to see him settled at his aunt's. Unfortunately this did not happen and two months passed. The solicitor gave his perception of the reason why matters dragged.

'I think it was fifty per cent a resource issue, probably forty per cent the social worker, 'I haven't got the time' and ten per cent bloody mindedness.'

Although there was no plan for Edward to attend the final hearing his behaviour did begin to be more disruptive at school. He had had a burst of bad behaviour in the week before the final hearing. The professionals decided that this reflected Edward's awareness that something was about to happen. He had had a number of visitors that week, including his mother, his guardian and his solicitor. After the final hearing, Edward became increasingly unsettled. The school said that he continually raised the fact that he was not happy having to sleep there. He also wanted more contact with his family. His behaviour deteriorated and the school considered excluding him.

As a result of Edward's behaviour, the local authority arranged for a taxi to take him back each night to sleep at his short-term foster carer's home. He was collected each morning by taxi and returned to school. Edward was delighted and his behaviour improved. By his behaviour Edward had achieved what his representatives had failed to do. As Edward had not yet moved, his guardian and solicitor decided to say their goodbyes to him at his short-term foster carer's. The research interview with Edward also took place there. The guardian felt that Edward's behaviour was directly related to the delay in placing him with his aunt.

'He has had some difficult times not knowing why things were not happening.'

Another school term passed before Edward moved to his aunt's home. He now lives with a sister and some cousins and attends a special school as a day pupil.

The young people subject to their mother's application for contact maintained the same agenda throughout the proceedings and afterwards. They did not want to have contact with their mother. The guardian's recommendation reflected the strong views held by the children although her investigations had led her to feel some sympathy for the mother. The guardian concluded that the children could not be forced to have such contact. On the day of the final hearing, the mother withdrew her application for contact. The consequence of this action was that there was no order made by the court. No representative requested that any order be made. As a result, there was neither an order for contact nor an order barring contact. The young people did not attend the hearing at court but were angry to learn that the court did not make an order for no contact. They now felt vulnerable. Their mother was free to make a similar future application which, in their view, would again disrupt their lives.

The young people's comments to the researcher reflected their anger.

'Like it seemed a big, big waste of time when, at the end, she just pulled out of it. I mean, if they're going to do it then they might as well go through with it instead of wasting our time, [the guardian's] time, your time and everybody else's time. She should have finished it but she didn't. I would have preferred an order that you don't have to see her. She wouldn't go ahead then.'

'I'm just a bit angry about that 'cause they put us all through it just for her to withdraw it.'

Indeed, it would have been possible for the solicitor for the children to take instructions to have the application dismissed without any hearing.

Two factors could have justified dismissing the application. The young people were adamant that they did not want contact and there had been no change in the plan for the children since the mother's contact was ended. Such children's rights-oriented action by the solicitor is problematic in that it would have precluded the guardian from investigating and putting forward her view of the children's interests. The guardian had taken the view that if the children had the opportunity to discuss the application in more detail, they might have become interested in renewing contact. As it happened, the children did not change their minds and the mother applied to withdraw her application. At that stage the solicitor for the children could have requested an order that the mother not be allowed to make a further contact application without the leave of the court under Children Act 1989, s. 91(14). Such action would have gone some way to allay the young people's concern about future applications.

Carl did not attend court but his aunt and mother did. The care order was discharged in favour of a residence order to his aunt. This order was made by agreement with the parties. Carl's guardian was unable to attend the final hearing as she was involved in a lengthy case in London. His solicitor was present at court. The social worker was also at court and asked Carl's aunt to tell him about the outcome. Carl was pleased as he was able to remain with his aunt.

Carl told the researcher that he had always wanted to stay with his aunt but felt that his social worker had pressurised him into returning to his mother. He did not feel able to voice this. He was worried by the discharge proceedings and decided to run away back to his aunt's. Had he seen his solicitor he would have explained his actions.

'Yes well I would have told her why I had run off and all that.'

Again the child's action, and not that of his representatives, had produced the desired outcome.

Richard was also made subject to a care order by agreement. He said he was unconcerned by this. He had wanted to attend the court hearing but his other concern had been whether he was to face criminal proceedings in respect of some issues. This matter had yet to be decided. He did not attend the final hearing of his care proceedings although he had originally asked to go and hear what was being said. His guardian had facilitated this but had explained to Richard that he would have to compromise and accept that he could only be present for part of the hearing. In the end Richard did not attend. He explained:

'I did but then I changed my mind. I had something better in school to do.'

James was detained in the secure unit under a two month secure accommodation order. He had not opposed the order. His agenda was still to get out of the unit as quickly as possible but he had accepted his solicitor's advice to be seen to work with the staff at the unit. At the court hearing mention was made of the need for James to be kept occupied, particularly throughout the school holidays, otherwise there was concern that he might reoffend. The making of the secure order coincided with this period with a plan that James should be fully rehabilitated back home by the end of August.

The researcher intended to interview James at the unit two weeks later but discovered that he had returned home. Neither his guardian nor his solicitor was aware that James had been released. The interview took place at his home in the presence of his mother. She dominated the interview. All James would say was that he wanted to forget all about the proceedings.

'Nothing good came out of it.'

James' solicitor commented upon the case. He felt that he had made little difference. He had felt that it was 'an overwhelming case for a secure accommodation order' but that he had been prepared to oppose it if that was what James had wanted. The solicitor said that he and the guardian had felt that James' home situation had much to do with his behaviour and that James probably had a yearning to have contact with his stepfather. He explained:

'We did our best to encourage him and it would have been a lot more beneficial to him if we had got him to have some contact with his stepfather, I think. That was just a muddle.'

Another unopposed secure accommodation order was made for Barbara. She had been in secure for many months and her solicitor now saw her as being institutionalised. She believed that Barbara was aware that the renewed orders ensured Barbara could remain at the unit and this gave her security whilst ensuring that Barbara retained the solicitor she valued as a friend. Barbara's guardian felt that Barbara wanted to be more independent but feared leaving the safety of the unit. Barbara told the researcher how she felt about the renewed order:

'Yes, obviously I didn't really want one but I did agree with it if you know what I mean. It's quite nice here actually.'

Barbara remained in the secure placement; she has become institutionalised. As she approaches age 18 and the time when she has to leave care, her solicitor is acutely concerned that there is no provision which will meet the needs created by the way she has been brought up in the public care system.

WHAT ABOUT YOUNG PEOPLE'S AGENDAS?

In the study there were no formal applications before the court by children or young people. In this respect the young people's concerns may have had less attention by the court. A guardian should raise the court's awareness to the child's wishes through their report, as should the solicitor for the child, acting on the guardian's instructions. It is a matter for the guardian's professional judgement whether to instruct a solicitor to challenge the local authority care plan. The guardian system emphasises independence over accountability, which means that if the guardian chooses not to highlight any matters on behalf of the child, they may remain unconsidered. In fact for the guardian, avoidance of conflict with social services departments may be the easier course to follow.

Although individual issues or cases could generate conflict with social workers, the social services department or local authority lawyers, guardians ad litem generally felt that their expertise was recognised within social services departments. This meant that it could be possible to influence the contents of the care plan.

> 'The guardian is in quite a significant position in that her views matter. Guardians are listened to compared to field social workers where the decision-making happens at conference, at Team Manager level. The social worker, I feel, is not always listened to.'

Both the solicitors and guardians tended to empathise with the field social worker, feeling that failures were the result of the pressures they worked under and the limited resources available. They were reluctant to increase the stress on social workers by complaining formally because they understood that they were subject to the resource constraints in the social services department.

> '. . . but they can't perform miracles. When you think about, I suppose the type of placement they have got to find, it may be difficult. I think that was what [the guardian] was saying. My immediate response was, "Well perhaps we should make a complaint because nothing has happened." But I think he [guardian] was looking at perhaps why things hadn't happened and it would be very difficult . . .'

Some guardians were concerned that challenges to a care plan would only bring conflict from the local authority and that if the care order is needed to protect the child, appearing to disagree with it, for whatever reason, undermined their credibility. As discussed earlier, the guardians and the solicitors for both Edward and William were willing to take a more proactive stance and challenge care plans irrespective of the consequences. Nevertheless, young people's agendas about where and with whom they would live, and contact, can remain easily hidden when they are left to be determined by the local authority.

Where adult parties raise these issues, they do become significant to the court. Adults can more easily make applications. Yet the young people in this study showed that their agendas reflected these same issues. They were live issues for the child. Children were not informed of the possibility of making applications about contact and placement, and children's concerns about contact were not necessarily even brought to the notice of the court. When they were raised whether by the guardian ad litem or the solicitor, this was within the context of the local authority care plan and the issues were viewed as under local authority control. In this respect they were not seen as major issues for the court. They were, however, major issues for young people.

CONCLUSION

Young people do not choose their guardians, most do not choose their solicitors. Children have to rely upon proactive guardians and solicitors to challenge local authority control whilst court proceedings are continuing. Even so, there are no guarantees that the court will agree to debate these issues. They may be buried as quickly as they surfaced. Guardians and solicitors were acutely aware of the limitations on the powers of the court and the pressures on the child's social worker. During their investigation, many tried to achieve improvements in children's situations, including possibly changes in the care plan, by liaising with social services. They saw negotiation and conciliation as key tools for improvement.

By the time of the final hearing, there was no conflict between the adult parties and the local authority in any of the study cases. In these contexts the guardian had limited opportunities to raise any outstanding concerns about the child's or young person's future care. In addition, raising issues at this point was seen as counter-productive, as it might only serve to delay the final order and increase conflict with social services. Where concerns remained unresolved after the final order, guardians and solicitors were powerless because their appointments had terminated. Goodbye visits to children and young people might provide one last opportunity to inform them of their rights but guardians and solicitors were only too aware that children could rarely take matters further on their own, and they were concerned not to be seen to undermine social services.

9

POLICY AND PRACTICE ISSUES

INTRODUCTION

The working of the current system gives no grounds for complacency. Children and young people involved in specified proceedings are vulnerable. They are anxious because of family breakdown and because the long-term arrangements for their care are uncertain. They are frequently isolated and have needs for care and support which are not being met. Neither children's interests nor their wishes are strenuously advocated by their representatives in every case. The court's limited powers mean that it is often unable to make decisions in the best interests of children but has to accept what appears to be the least unsatisfactory outcome.

As part of the process of developing an understanding of lawyers' approaches to working with guardians ad litem in representing children and young people in public law proceedings, the authors discussed their preliminary findings with guardians ad litem, solicitors and researchers with experience in the fields of socio-legal studies and child care. Draft copies of the research findings were sent to 15 experienced solicitors and meetings were held to discuss the research with the Representing Children subgroup of the Solicitors Family Law Association and the Childcare subcommittee of the Law Society. Solicitors from Lawyers for Children also attended this meeting.

The Solicitors Family Law Association is a membership organisation for solicitors with a special interest in family law and a commitment to a conciliatory approach to family disputes (SFLA 1984). The SFLA organises local and national training for solicitors and provides written guidance for solicitors acting for children. The Association of Lawyers for Children runs an annual conference focusing on child care law (ALC 1996, 1998). The Law Society is both the representative body for solicitors and the regulator of the solicitors' profession. It established and administers the Children Panel, the accreditation system for solicitors who act for children in public law cases. It provides guidance to solicitors acting for children (Liddle 1992; Law Society 1994, 1994a). All three organisations regularly contribute to policy development in the area of child law.

The initial response of all the lawyers at these meetings was that the study had observed bad practice. The label *bad practice* may be applied in two distinct ways, to the failings of individual practitioners, or to the way the system operates. The distinction is important; selection, training and increased accountability can improve individual practice but will not solve structural problems.

Within each meeting individual solicitors criticised the study solicitors for deferring to their guardians ad litem, for not taking instructions from Sylvia, for failing to ensure that the care plan for Peter named his carers and for not getting Edward his skateboard. However, as discussion developed, it became increasingly clear that practice on such issues varied widely and that most of the practices observed would have been followed by some of those present. Solicitors did vary their approach to fit with the requirements of guardians ad litem, although none had ever met a guardian who insisted on accompanying them whenever they saw a child. They did not routinely introduce barristers to older child clients; one solicitor commented that guardians ad litem did not want this. Nor did they always discuss with older children whether they wanted the opportunity to attend the hearing. They did not necessarily ensure that they or the guardian attended case conferences or other similar meetings held by the local authority.

Only in relation to the obligation to take instructions from Sylvia did all the solicitors agree that they would have acted differently. But they were commenting without the opportunity to assess her competence and suggested different ages when instructions could be taken. One said it was his practice to take instructions from all older children regardless of whether the child was in conflict with the guardian ad litem and another routinely wrote to the other parties when acting for children over the age of 11 years, warning them that she might have to take instructions from the child direct.

A recurrent theme in these discussions was diversity of practice. Individual guardians approached cases differently, as did local authorities, the courts and different judges. Their knowledge of local practices necessarily affected the way experienced solicitors handled cases, magnifying differences between cases rather than imposing standardisation. For example, one local authority might expect to provide full details of the care plan, including identifying the carers, whereas others were unwilling or unable to do so. Similarly, where information about the care plan was missing, in some courts it was possible with considerable pressure to obtain an adjournment or even a witness summons for the director of social services. But in others, the details of the child's care were regarded as a matter for the local authority alone or the pressure to avoid delay was overwhelming where it was clear, as for Peter, that there was no alternative to a care order. In this context William's representatives should be congratulated for their efforts to ensure that the decision about the funding to secure his care plan was taken before the final hearing.

Although diversity in practice may indicate a responsive system it is also a characteristic of one which is arbitrary. It appeared that diversity in care proceedings could allow experienced practitioners to achieve the best for their young clients but could also disempower children who generally lacked easy access to accurate information about how the system operated. Even their solicitor and guardian ad litem might be unable to predict how an issue would be handled.

There was general agreement amongst the solicitors that the court had very limited powers, particularly where the case for a care order was obvious. Although the court could influence the information available to it by ordering assessments, it could not determine how the child was cared for by the local authority once a care order had been made. The lack of power over the child's fate inhibited some courts from putting pressure on the local authority, possibly because they recognised that there was no advantage to the child in clarifying the care plan if it need not be implemented. It also affected the opportunity that solicitors for children or young people had to exert pressure during the proceedings and the way they approached disputes about the care plan.

Although the solicitors emphasised individual failings of the representatives in the study, it became increasingly clear that many of the practices the researchers observed also occurred outside the areas where the research was conducted. The solicitors' labelling of the way cases were handled as 'bad practice', for example the uncertainty about the plans for Peter, Sylvia, Martin and Edward, did not mean that they would have been able to achieve a better result in courts where they worked. Their practice had to take account of the pressures on the local authority social services department concerned and reflect the attitude and the approach of the court.

The solicitors did not identify other general constraints on their practice. They were keen to stress that they were 'not in it for the money' and determined how a case should be handled from the circumstances, the facts, the child, the guardian, the local authority and the court, not because of constraints on their use of time. The recent emphasis of the Legal Aid Board on the need to justify litigation costs, even in cases where legal aid is available without a means or merit test (Legal Aid Board 1997), may have placed them under new constraints but was not raised by the solicitors in discussion.

It appeared that some of the 'bad practice' was inherent to the system. Individual solicitors and guardians had to work within the system and despite their professional independence they had only limited opportunities to influence the way the system responded to their young clients. Their practice was particularly dependent on the attitude and approach of the judges and magistrates. In addition, where solicitors repeatedly worked with the same few guardians, the pressure to conform to the guardian's approach was strong and professional independence was reduced. The so-licitors who practised in London said that this was not an issue for them because of the size of the panel and the area it covered but some acknowl-edged that they were regularly instructed by the same few guardians. In a similar way, the guardian's outlook could be narrowed and their indepen-dence undermined by repeated exposure to the approach of one local authority.

Plans to change the system for representing children and training for all those who work within it need to be informed by the views and experience of children caught up in it. Reform of children's representation in public law proceedings and its extension to private law proceedings should take account of the uneven distributions of power between adults and children, lawyers and social work professionals, local authorities and courts. Although individ-uals make a difference, the quality of service which is provided generally depends on the structures and relationships between all involved.

THE ORGANISATION OF THE GALRO SERVICE

In February 1998, the Home Secretary announced that consideration was being given to establishing a unified court welfare service which would include the Family Court Welfare Service, currently provided through the Probation Service, the GALRO service, provided by local GALRO panels administered by local authorities, and the Official Solicitor, an Officer of the Supreme Court appointed by the Lord Chancellor. The review was being conducted with a view to identifying the potential for efficiency savings (Hoon 1998) but the idea that court welfare services should be amalgamated had been raised in the 1980s (Murch and Hooper 1992). In July 1980 a consultation paper was issued (DH et al 1998).

Although all three services provide reports for the courts and both guardians ad litem and the Official Solicitor represent children in family proceedings, there are major differences in the staffing and organisation of these three services. Whereas those undertaking investigation work as guardians ad litem or court welfare officers are professionally qualified in social work, caseworkers from the Official Solicitor's office are mostly civil servants with a background in courts administration. One consequence of the lack of professional expertise in the Official Solicitor's office has been the frequent use of experts, particularly child psychiatrists, to carry out assessments of the child (Masson 1992). Both the court welfare service and the Official Solicitor's office are cash limited, managed services. A finite sum is provided for the services each year. In the Family Court Welfare Service this can mean that managers are unable to respond promptly, or at all, to requests from the court. The Official Solicitor only acts in a restricted class of cases and appointments are always subject to his consent (*Practice Note* 1993). Staff in these services are accountable to their managers for their work. The GALRO service itself is managed, but individual guardians are not subject to any control or supervision in the work they do. Guardians are accountable to the court, which has the power to replace them in an individual case. The panel is required to ensure that guardians are available whenever required by the courts but cannot manage its resources by limiting the amount of work done by guardians (1992 *R. v. Cornwall C.C. ex p. G.*).

Before a unified structure could be established it would be necessary to agree qualification standards for the staff. Unless current distinctions were to be maintained between public law and private law cases, all staff would need substantial training in the area of practice in which they have no experience. A unified service could have some advantages over the current arrangements for the guardian ad litem service. Its separation from local authorities would clarify its independence from those involved in proceedings. Professional management would allow for the supervision of guardians, removing variations in practice with the potential for raising standards to those provided by the best guardians and increasing accountability. But there may be disadvantages, particularly if there is strong pressure to drive down costs. The greater demand for welfare reports in private law cases may divert resources away from the provision of guardians and lead to delays in appointment. Expertise derived from working on complex public law cases may be wasted if guardians are assigned to private law work.

The creation of a unified court welfare service also raises the questions how to provide and pay for the necessary legal services. Both the GALRO service and the Official Solicitor's department are major users of legal services; these too are provided in different ways. The Official Solicitor is his own solicitor, i.e. there is an *in house* legal service, whereas guardians appoint solicitors who nominally act for the child and are funded by legal aid. Only where the child is separately represented do the guardian's legal costs fall on the panel (and thus on the local authority). The appropriateness of treating the lawyer who acts for the guardian as the child's representative is discussed below. Bringing legal services within the new court welfare service would shift decisions about the use of legal services from individual guardians and the Legal Aid Board to the managers of the court welfare system. Those who made decisions about provision of legal services would have responsibility for delivering a timely service for the courts. It would allow for a different balance between expenditure on legal and guardian services. However, if the new service were to be reponsible for legal services to guardians there would need to be a substantial transfer of resources from the Legal Aid Board.

REPRESENTATION OF CHILDREN BY GUARDIANS AND SOLICITORS

When the Children Act 1989 was under consideration, discussions about the need for both a solicitor and a guardian for every child in care proceedings focused on the shortage of guardians which then existed in some areas, the cost of dual representation and the problems of identifying cases where guardians were required. The use of a selective approach to appointing guardians which had existed prior to the Children Act 1989 was criticised by the Law Society and voluntary organisations. Murch, who had extensively researched court practice and the views of lawyers and guardians, concluded that the partnership between guardian and solicitor did substantially improve the position of children in care proceedings but he was prepared to consider representation by guardian alone in the first instance, provided guardians had access to legal advice (Murch et al 1990, 46).

More recently, Lord Irvine, before he was appointed as Lord Chancellor, questioned the necessity for a solicitor where the guardian supports the local authority's case (Irvine 1997). The question was repeated by the Minister in an address to the National Association for Guardians ad litem and Reporting Officers which reflected on the difference of approach to investigation and children's representation in public and private child law (Hoon 1997). The Advisory Board on Family Law, established to advise the Lord Chancellor on the implementation of the Family Law Act 1996, has started to consider whether Family Law Act 1996, s. 64, the provision which allows for separate representation for children in private law cases, should be implemented. The inference from the consultation document is that there may be room for some trade-off – providing increased representation in private law at the expense of reduced representation in public law cases (DH et al 1998, para. 1.31).

The withdrawal of legal representation in public law cases is strongly opposed by the National Association for Guardians ad litem and Reporting Officers, which has argued that removal of the child's lawyer would prevent the child having parity with other parties, undermine the guardian's capacity to act in the child's best interests and place too great demands on guardians who have not been trained as lawyers (Collier 1997; Jackson 1997; Hamilton 1997). Proponents of legal representation for the child and guardian in these cases emphasise the solicitor's role as advocate for the guardian, as an adviser on law and procedure and, in cases where the young person is competent to instruct the solicitor and wishes to do so, as the young person's advocate (ALC 1998). There is no doubt these are functions for solicitors and that guardians' training and experience does not equip them to argue legal points nor to cross-examine witnesses. However, these skills are not required *throughout* every case; contested hearings occur in only a minority of cases, although many cases are disputed at some stage. Seventy per cent of cases involve children below the age of 10 years (DH 1995c) and so the question of the child's competence and hence the possibility of giving separate instructions does not arise.

Guardians are increasingly involved in the appointment and instruction of experts, sometimes for the child alone but often on behalf of all the parties. This may involve negotiating and writing detailed instructions, a task usually performed by the child's solicitor with the assistance of proformas (CAAC 1997a). Negotiation is increasingly important, so it is more pertinent to ask whether guardians should be expected to undertake this even though other parties are negotiating through lawyers and the issues under consideration relate to the legal process. In part the answer may depend on the infrastructure of the guardian ad litem service and the extent to which guardians have access to legal advice.

Negotiation or advocacy?

Before the Children Act the extent to which negotiation was acceptable in care cases was unclear. Macleod noted that 'In care proceedings where the primary purpose must be to secure the child's welfare, the middle ground open for compromise is less apparent'. Nevertheless, she found that a third of children's solicitors and two-fifths of parents' lawyers had been involved in some negotiations in the sample case. Discussions related to the conduct of the case and to its outcome. By trying to establish what parties could agree to, a solicitor might encourage a reconsideration of their position so that 'what started as a discussion could end as a compromise settlement' (Macleod 1989, 72). Some guardians were critical of what might seem like bargaining over a child's future, particularly where this happened at the door of the court.

The partnership approach introduced by the Children Act 1989 has encouraged local authorities to work harder to gain parental cooperation and to avoid compulsory measures. Fears have been expressed that too much emphasis has been placed on parental wishes to the detriment of children's welfare (Bainham 1990, 221) and that in the face of parental agreement the courts may overlook the child's wishes (White et al 1995, 32). Within proceedings, the partnership approach, negative views of adversarialism, the 'no order' principle and case management have combined to make negotiation a more accepted part of child care practice. In addition, the Legal Aid Board requires assisted parties to behave reasonably in litigation and expects them to have attempted to negotiate matters such as contact before bringing proceedings (Legal Aid Board 1997). Courts expect parties to come to agreement about the selection, appointment and instruction of experts (CAAC 1997a, 25), agreements about interim care orders or procedural matters avoid the necessity for interim hearings. The courts have even accepted that it may be appropriate to proceed to make an order on the basis that the parents accept that an order is necessary and admit that the child is suffering significant harm, even though they deny major parts of the allegations against them (*Stockport M.B.C. v. D.* 1995). Negotiation has become an integral part of the proceedings.

Negotiation has considerable advantages over litigation. It may produce better outcomes for all the parties, particularly where it allows for flexible solutions which could not easily be formalised by the orders set out in the Children Act, outcomes which have the strong support of the parties, or real cooperation to make arrangements work. However, negotiation may provide inadequate protection for weaker parties, produce coerced agreements which fail because they are not accepted or lead to outcomes which compromise the child's welfare. Whatever the impact in individual cases, negotiation leads to a marginalisation of the court (Hunt and Macleod 1997, 275).

The increased emphasis on negotiation rather than litigation in child care cases necessitates a reconsideration of representation and the skills required by all the professionals involved. Social workers do seek to negotiate with parents. In some cases which proceed to court negotiation has failed; in some others, the local authority is seeking an order to confirm the agreed arrangement. In many cases which result in court applications there has been a substantial period of social services involvement with the family (Hunt and Macleod 1997); in these cases the lack or breakdown of cooperative relationships between social workers and families means that protective measures cannot be relied on and, consequently, organisational concerns about risks to children cannot be contained. Although an application may help to produce change, the social worker who has been unable to establish parental cooperation is not in a strong position to negotiate when proceedings are started. Moreover, local authority organisation rarely gives the social worker with case responsibility power to negotiate outcomes, particularly where there are resource issues. No social services manager may be present at court to negotiate there, leaving late settlements in the hands of the local authority lawyer.

If the local authority's negotiator is a solicitor, guardians expect the child's solicitor to negotiate on their behalf. Consequently, lawyers have tended to dominate pre-court negotiation because of their experience and style (Riches 1997). But only a guardian or social worker can make direct contact with the parents or other parties because of the professional requirement that a solicitor contacts another solicitor's client through their solicitor. Negotiation via the parents' solicitor may safeguard parents from pressure but evidence of limited knowledge and understanding of law and practice in this area on the part of some solicitors who act for parents (Murch et al 1990, 25; Lindley 1994; Freeman 1994; Hunt and Macleod 1997) suggests that many are not in a strong position to do this or to advise their clients about possible ways forward.

The guardians' greater knowledge about social services provision, better understanding of the child's needs and wishes and clear professional commitment to safeguarding the welfare of the child provide them with a strong basis from which to negotiate an outcome in the child's best interests. Their independence, at least if it is accepted by all the other parties, may increase the chances of negotiations succeeding. The conflict between the guardian's role as an adviser to the court and a representative of the child is no greater in negotiation than in other forms of representation. Some guardians will need further training before they feel equipped to play a greater part in negotiation. Lawyers will still be necessary to negotiate some procedural issues and will remain involved in negotiations for other parties.

Party status for children

Party status for children is said to be important because it places the children on the same footing as other parties. This research has shown that in reality even older children are not equal parties. Where an adult acts on behalf of a child the individual child can be lost from sight. Children's access to their solicitor is generally mediated through the guardian and children have no direct access to the court; their litigation is conducted on their behalf. Most have little or no access to the statements of other parties or assessments and reports which relate to them. Solicitors do not usually attend case conferences on behalf of their child clients but they would attend if acting for parents. Solicitors stated that they may agree to attend a case conference if the guardian is unable to attend and requests that they do so on the guardian's behalf. However, in contrast with their parents, children are privileged by having additional representation by a social work expert with rights of access to the local authority's files. Sonia, the young parent in secure accommodation, was greatly helped by her representatives arranging that she should also have a panel guardian in the care proceedings relating to her baby daughter. Equality is not the point; the system seeks to ensure that the court has all the necessary information about the child and gives paramount consideration to the child's interests as determined by it, following representations to it by all the parties.

Representation of children and young people in these proceedings is largely based on shielding them from the process rather than assisting them to participate. Consequently, their party status does not help to make the proceedings real for them. Greater opportunities to participate, where they wished to do so, might encourage some children to engage with the proceedings. It would also necessitate changes in court practice, such as clearer use of language, shorter hearings and more attention to the needs of ordinary people, which would also benefit parents, relatives and carers.

It has also been suggested that the child's party status helps to ensure that all involved concentrate on the child as an individual person. The focus on the child or young person is crucial. In most cases he or she is known only to a few of the participants in the proceedings, principally the parents, some of the social work professionals, the guardian ad litem and the solicitor for the child. Even these professionals may have known the child or young person for a short time and seen him or her on a comparatively few occasions. Other witnesses may have seen the child; for the remaining participants, including the judge, magistrates or barristers, the child is a stranger, illustrated by the statements and reports of others. Unless this information makes the child real there is a danger that those deciding the issues will see him or her as just a case and lose sight of the human consequences of their decision. Indeed, where options are limited or unsatisfactory they may prefer not to think too much about the consequences for the child or young person.

This consequence of distancing children from the proceedings appears unlikely to benefit them. Action needs to be taken to counteract it. Requiring the child's attendance, as occurred in the magistrates' courts for children over the age of 5 years before the Children Act 1989, would be disruptive to children's lives and oppressive to those who did not wish to attend. But ensuring that reports contained a pen picture of each child and that a photograph of the child is in the court throughout the proceedings could help to remind everyone whose life they were talking about.

Party status has not guaranteed that the court retains a focus on the child as it should. But it has permitted the guardian to make applications in the proceedings and to appeal as other parties can. Currently welfare officers who carry out investigations and provide reports in private law proceedings concerning children cannot do this. If the court is to have an inquisitorial role it is crucial that the person appointed to investigate for it can make applications in appropriate cases.

Lawyers for children or guardians

From the institution of the system of dual representation, both solicitors and guardians have repeatedly stated that they gain support from each other's presence (Macleod 1989, 27, 33). It is less clear that young children derive any greater benefit from having their own solicitor than from representation by a guardian with access to legal advice. The current practice of solicitors visiting children briefly, only once or twice, does not provide the child with proper opportunities to understand the solicitor's role nor to gain confidence in him or her. These visits have more to do with beliefs that the solicitor will be a better representative for a child if he or she can picture a child and that meeting the child, rather than seeing a photograph, is essential to this process.

Similarly, the practice of children only seeing their solicitor with the guardian provides mutual support for the adult professionals but does not help the child put forward a view independent of the guardian.

Although party status and representation by a panel guardian ad litem and solicitor provides a structure for highly skilled representation of both children's wishes and their interests, in practice, the system delivers less than it promises. Solicitors are dependent on guardians, they find it difficult to establish a relationship with their child clients, spend comparatively little time with children or young people on their own and are reluctant to take instructions from them directly.

Representation for older children

Changes in solicitors' practice could strengthen the system for children and young people. The fact that the majority of children are too young to use a lawyer's services directly may mean that solicitors' style of practice in these cases has developed with younger children in mind. Older children could benefit from a solicitor who explained the process to them, discussed with them their participation in it and helped them to understand the proposals of the other parties. They lose out when solicitors defer to guardians, expect that young people will not participate and assume that the direct work with child clients will be undertaken by the guardian. Solicitors need more training to enable them to deal confidently with young people and most need to spend more time with young clients if they are to treat them *as clients*. Solicitors will have to be able to relate directly to young people who are their clients in order to assist them to give instructions.

At present, solicitors are only required to take their instructions from the child in specified proceedings if he or she is competent to give instructions and wishes to give instructions which conflict with those of the guardian ad litem (FPR r. 4.12(1)(a)). There are two major problems with this. The competence test gives too much discretion to the solicitor whose professional background rarely provides an adequate basis for the decision. It is not appropriate for solicitors to seek advice from the guardian because there is a clear conflict of interest. Interviews with solicitors indicated general agreement amongst them about the factors which should be considered, but not about their application (Sawyer 1995, 185). Sawyer suggested that solicitors were really concerned whether children's best interests were served by direct involvement in the proceedings, not whether they were competent (Sawyer 1995, 189). The courts' negative approach to children as litigants may influence them. Even where the child would be judged competent he or she may not be given the opportunity to instruct the solicitor. Failure by the solicitor to discuss fully with the child the plan and the basis for it, or to ensure the child is adequately informed about the court's powers and has the opportunity to make their concerns known, means that the solicitor remains unaware of conflict between the child's and the guardian's points of view. These difficulties would be overcome if the competence test were replaced by a presumption of competence at a specific age and all older children were represented by a solicitor under an obligation to take their instructions from the outset.

There is clearly no right age for a presumption of competence; many different age tests already apply in English law (Cretney and Masson 1997, 575). Children can be held criminally liable for their actions at age 10 but until 1998 there was a rebuttable presumption that they lacked criminal intent below the age of 14 years. The Children (Scotland) Act contains a presumption that children of 12 years or more have sufficient maturity to form a view about major decisions in their lives (s. 6(1)). The consent of a child of 12 is also required for the child's adoption in Scotland (Adoption (Scotland) Act 1978, s. 12(8)). Setting the age too low and thus providing representation for children who are not capable of using it would be wasteful, but setting it too high would deny young people an opportunity for active participation in the proceedings.

Lawyers need to be skilled in communicating with their clients so that they can help them to identify their concerns and give instructions. This is particularly true where the client is a young person without previous experience of using lawyers and the proceedings are complex or emotive. Mechanisms would be needed to cover the situations where the presumption did not lead to an appropriate procedure. A lawyer who was unable to take instructions from a young person would have to inform the court and be replaced. If a younger child needed representation separate from the guardian, for example because he or she objected to the guardian, he or she would be able to apply to the court for representation.

Separation of the young person's lawyer from the guardian service would remove the possibility of cosy solicitor–guardian relationships interfering with the young person's wish to understand and participate (to whatever extent) in the proceedings. The solicitor would be responsible for explaining the process to the young person, ensuring that their views were properly explained to the court (by the solicitor or by the guardian) and that the young person was properly informed about the outcome of the proceedings.

Representation for younger children

If such a system were adopted, the representation of younger children would be entirely in the hands of the guardian ad litem who would have access to legal services. This would largely reflect current practice but instead of lawyers being drawn from private practice and appointed by individual guardians on a case-by-case basis they would be appointed to the unified court welfare service. As the sole representative of the child, the guardian would have to take full responsibility for ensuring that the child understood to the best of their ability what was being decided and was able to contribute to the decision. Young children would not meet or interact with the guardian's lawyer.

The future of the Children Panel for solicitors

Providing legal services to guardians primarily through solicitors appointed for the court welfare service has implications for the Law Society Children Panel, particularly for retention of a pool of experienced solicitors in private practice who could represent young people. Lawyers undergo training and interview in order to join the Children Panel, and membership enables them to access an additional stream of work; if this stream were to be reduced, the Children Panel would cease to be as attractive and might dwindle in size as solicitors decided against joining or renewing their membership. In consequence, it might be more difficult to find solicitors to act for children or young people in either public law or private law children cases. A renamed Children Panel could acquire a new role by taking over the representation of parents from general practice. This would necessitate changes to membership criteria and to training. The new name should reflect the groups the panel serves, young people, parents and others.

The establishment of the Children Panel both identified and helped to create solicitors with specialist knowledge of this work. Parents have at least as much need for good representation as guardians and are less able to assess the quality of what they are provided with. Restricting parents to representation by specialist practitioners might be controversial in the legal profession, despite considerable evidence of the inadequate representation provided to some parents (Murch and Hooper 1992; Lindley 1994; Freeman 1994; CAAC 1995; Booth and Booth 1996; Hunt and Macleod 1997) and the fact that the cost of representation is paid by legal aid. Changes to legal aid are likely to restrict assisted parties' choice of solicitor. Restrictions run counter to the notion that the right to representation includes the right to choose freely which lawyer acts as the representative. It is, however, difficult to see that free choice should be viewed as a protection of the individual litigant when it allows choice of the less than competent, particularly where this may advantage the State.

STANDARDISATION OF LEGAL PROCEEDINGS

The Children Act 1989 formally established a system for triple jurisdiction in family proceedings so that cases could be allocated to the most appropriate level of court for their complexity but would be heard under the same procedure in courts with the same powers. This largely remains the case although the High Court which retains its inherent jurisdiction can make orders that are outside the powers of the lower courts and has claimed the right to hear specific types of case, particularly applications for private law orders by children (*Re S.* 1993; *President's Direction* 1993). Although the basic elements of court procedure are set out in Court Rules, the ways courts operate in practice have long been known to vary from court to court (Hilgendorf 1981; Masson, Norbury and Chatterton 1984; Murch et al 1990). There was some attempt to streamline practice with the implementation of the Children Act 1989 through the establishment of the Children Act Advisory Committee, with a remit to monitor practice and procedure under the Act, and local Family Court Business Committees. However, courts retain wide discretion over the way proceedings are to be conducted, to the extent that there is said to be a 'spectrum of procedure for family cases from the ex parte application on minimal evidence to the full and detailed investigations on oral evidence which may be prolonged' (*Re B.* 1994, Butler-Sloss L.J.). The form of hearing is a matter for the judge's discretion. Whether the child is permitted (or required) to attend is also a matter for the court to decide (Children Act 1989, s. 95). These wide powers enable the judge to tailor the proceedings to fit the circumstances or the case, for example, dismissing applications which appear to be without merit without any oral hearing (*Cheshire C.C. v. M.* 1993). However, they also mean that there is considerable variation from court to court in the way cases are handled. Concern has been expressed that too much hangs on the attitude of individual judges (Lyon and Parton 1995). This makes it difficult for professionals who are not familiar with the particular culture of a court to advise clients and also makes it impossible to provide a clear and accurate account of court process for the young people and parents involved. It can also cause confusion, particularly where different hearings in the same case are taken by different judges, as is common, and those judges countermand directions given by previous judges.

Information for children and young people

Children and young people would benefit if they had access to written information about the roles and responsibilities of their representatives and the court, the relationship between the court proceedings and having a social worker and the part that they can play in the different decisions which are being taken about them. Although oral explanations are necessary, the complexity and newness of the information together with the stress of the situation means that it is unrealistic to expect these to provide sufficient explanations for children. Children can return to written information when they want to and get clarification from their carers, who are likely to be more confident helping a child to understand a leaflet than giving their own explanation. However, the current variations in practice by guardians ad litem, solicitors, and in the courts make it impossible to provide clear, accurate and detailed written information for children.

Whether or not the guardian ad litem service is to develop the way outlined above, work needs to be done to clarify the service provided to children and young people by guardians and solicitors. Children and young people involved in these proceedings should not have to rely on knowing the right question to ask, or asking the right person in order to find out what their rights are. A first step would be the provision of information packs for children of different ages (and the carers of younger children) which sets out clearly what they can expect from their guardian and solicitor. Comparable material has already been developed for child witnesses in criminal proceedings (NSPCC 1993). Many panels have devised leaflets which guardians may choose to use. Leaving the decision whether and how to explain the process to individual guardians has left some children with inadequate oral accounts.

Clear rules such as those proposed above for the representation of children of specific ages and the division of responsibility between guardians and solicitors would make it easier to explain to children (parents and social workers), how the child will be represented. Currently this is not possible even on a panel-by-panel basis. Full information covering the court proceedings could only be provided if there was greater standardisation there too.

Children's and young people's attendance at court

It was clear from the interviews with professionals that the courts' negative attitude towards the attendance of children and young people at their proceedings inhibited full discussion with them about their participation in the court process. This was a contributory factor in the non-engagement with the process of some young people, for example Tom and Alan. Young people do not want to be forced to attend but some would like the opportunity to do so, particularly to convey their wishes and to hear the decision. Concerns about protecting children from the long and acrimonious proceedings do not justify excluding children from short uncontested hearings. Better decisions about children's involvement at hearings can be made once the format of the hearing has become clear.

Opportunities for children's (limited) participation could be provided by adopting the system used in some European countries where proceedings involving children include an appointment for the child at the court. This provides a set time, enabling the child's attendance to be managed and allows the child an opportunity to see those involved and to make a brief statement if he or she wishes to do so. Such a system could easily be described in leaflets for children about the proceedings. Unlike the system which existed in the magistrates' court before the implementation of the Children Act 1989, it is intended to meet the child's needs to see the court not the court's wish to see the child. Consequently, reluctant children have the right to decide not to attend.

CARE PLANS AND THE POWER OF THE COURTS

Lack of court power to determine how or even whether a care plan is implemented limited discussion between the local authority and the other parties, including the guardian, about the content of the care plan. Thus Peter's guardian did not seek to find out exactly what arrangements were proposed for his care under the inevitable care order and Martin's representatives decided against delaying the proceedings and pressing social services to identify how his care plan would be implemented.

Representation of children's interests and wishes before the court would be more effective if the court had greater powers over the arrangements for care provided by the local authority, a proposal also made by Hunt and Macleod following their research into care proceedings (Hunt and Macleod 1997). Clearly the court's power over the local authority must be limited so that local authorities retain control over the majority of their child care resources which are needed for the larger number of cases which never come before the courts. However, this need to retain control would not appear to justify major changes in, or failure to implement within a reasonable time, the care plan which the local authority had put before the court as a basis for its care order. If courts were to get greater powers in respect of care plans, it might also be appropriate for them to have the power to deal with these matters by way of undertakings. The practical effect of the two forms should make little difference when ordered against a public body but the use of undertakings could reinforce the practice of seeking agreed solutions. Where undertakings were being accepted from parents, for example under the powers added by the Family Law Act 1996 to exclude alleged perpetrators from the child's home (Children Act 1989, ss. 38B, 44B), it is desirable for the court to be able to deal with the local authority similarly.

Whether or not the courts are given more power they need better and more timely information about the local authority's proposal (Thorpe and Clarke 1998). Where the care plan is determined by findings at the proof stage of the proceedings, either the hearing should be split or the local authority should provide separate plans to take account of the conflicting views put to the court. Children (and other parties) cannot give their views on the care plan unless they have an opportunity to know what it is in good time for the final hearing. This would be facilitated if the format of the care plan were set out in Court Rules, not just in guidance, and if the local authority were required to file it with the court (i.e. inform all the parties to the proceedings) well before the guardian has to file the report. Where matters remain outstanding, for example the child's placement has not been finalised or a new school has to be found, this should be stated explicitly so that it is clear to the child, the child's representatives and the court to what extent the child's concerns and those of the guardian are or are not met. This would also allow parents to be told exactly what the local authority had and had not decided.

As the child's representative the guardian (or the solicitor for an older child) should also have responsibility for ensuring that local authorities make appropriate arrangements for the child's care, education and contact during the proceedings as well as in the final care plan. Almost all the children interviewed for this study were preoccupied with their current situation; while their current concerns were not addressed they found it difficult to consider the future. It also appears to the researchers a poor use of scarce resources to appoint experts to assess children and lawyers to represent them if their basic requirements for care, education and social contact are not being met. Responsibility cannot be imposed on the child's representatives unless they also have some power in respect of these matters. They could have a statutory duty to refer matters to the local authority complaints system; alternatively, the court could be given a general obligation to safeguard the welfare of all children involved in these proceedings and the power to direct action by the local authority during the proceedings. Currently such a power only exists in relation to assessments where the child is the subject of an interim care or supervision order (Children Act 1989, s. 35(6); *Re C.* 1997).

Contact

Although the court is required by s. 34(11) of the Children Act 1989 to consider arrangements for contact between the child and parents, guardians and those with parental responsibility, this duty does not cover arrangements for contact with other relatives, for example siblings, and friends who have not obtained leave to seek a contact order. The emphasis on promotion of contact and the duty on the local authority under Children Act 1989, sched. 2, para. 15 is broader, 'to endeavour to promote contact between the child . . . and any relative, friend or other person connected with him'.

Children are frequently concerned to maintain contact with people who are not parties to the proceedings, including brothers and sisters who may not be able to obtain leave because of their immaturity or lack of access to advice. The court's and the guardian's duty should both be widened to reflect the duty to promote contact and to require consideration of arrangements for contact between the child and anyone with whom the child has expressed an interest in maintaining or renewing contact. Solicitors representing young people should always consider whether their client should make an application for contact in such cases. Where the court considers that contact which is not currently occurring would be in the child's best interest, it should have the power to accept undertakings or make orders requiring the local authority to facilitate this.

OTHER PRACTICE ISSUES

Case conferences

Attending case conferences is a useful way for the child's representative to establish the information held by and perspectives of other parties, particularly the local authority. Some meetings may also provide opportunities for representatives to put forward the child's perspective or their view of the child's interests. Parents' representatives find attending these meetings advantageous. The statement in *Working Together* (DH 1991a) which stresses that guardians ad litem can only be observers at such meetings appears to have discouraged their attendance to the potential disadvantage of children. Increased emphasis on negotiated arrangements makes it more important than ever that children's, young people's and parents' representatives should have the fullest access to the processes through which the local authority formulates its plans for action. It is vital that these processes are fully informed not only by the professionals' views but by those of the child or young person and their parents, and also that children, representatives and parents are aware as soon as possible of the proposed arrangements for care. Guardians ad litem should have no lesser status than parents; both local authorities and guardians will need to make sure that their approach to one another does not give the impression of a collusive relationship or lack of independence from the local authority on the part of the guardian. Either of these would be likely to undermine parental confidence and make it more difficult for the guardian to negotiate arrangements in the child's interests. The attendance of a solicitor for a young person should ensure that the young person's perspective is fully considered in any plans that are made. Encouraging representation and negotiation at this stage can improve the decisions reached and reduce conflict in the proceedings.

Children's access to the guardian ad litem's report

The children interviewed for this research were generally not satisfied with the limited access they were given to the guardian ad litem's report. Tom, Sylvia and William each commented negatively on their guardian's failure to show them the report. Indeed, this was the main criticism the children had of the guardian's action on their behalf. Children need full access to the report if they are going to make representations about its content or omissions either to the guardian or to the court through separate representation. Barbara suggested that the report should be countersigned by older children to indicate that they had read and understood it. At the Association of Lawyers for Children annual conference in 1998 one experienced solicitor stated that his practice was to indicate to the guardian that he would show their report in full to young people he was representing. As his clients they had a right to be fully informed. The onus was then on the guardian to seek a direction against this disclosure of the report. The response of other solicitors present was one of surprise; they had not considered doing this and considered disclosure of the report to the child was a matter for the guardian. In the ensuing debate these solicitors began to re-evaluate their practice in recognition of young people's rights. Some children and young people may even be able to police the implementation of the guardian's recommendations by asking their social worker, a reviewing officer or a children's rights officer what progress has been made on a particular issue. This may seem far fetched or an inappropriate burden to place on young people in the care system, but for some this may be the only way of ensuring their interests are being considered when change of personnel and of placement have left them without easy access to any professional who is well-informed about the proceedings which brought them into care. Moreover, children's requests may sometimes be more persuasive than those of other professionals or family members (Masson, Harrison and Pavlovic 1997).

The guardian's report is an important record for the child of a state of affairs at a particular time; children should have the right to retain the document for their personal information as other parties do. If there is no other way of providing secure storage for the future, as may be the case with a young child in care, this could be achieved by retaining a sealed copy in the child's social services file for access by the child alone.

Children's limited access to the report is also a factor in their confusion about other people's access to information in the report. The children in the study knew that the guardian was preparing a report for the court; some appeared not to be aware that the report would be seen by the other parties. Guardians need to take particular care to ensure that children do not think what they are saying is for the guardian and the judge alone. Again this misunderstanding could be minimised by ensuring that children were given clear written information about the process.

Knowing what has been decided

Although children may be too young to understand all or any of the consequences of the court's decision it can never be in the child's interests that the outcome is concealed from them, despite the inference that that may be the case in the National Standards for Guardians (DH 1996, 77). All the children in the study were aware that decisions were to be made about them by the court. Their anxiety to know the decision was not reflected in clear arrangements to convey to them, without delay, what had been decided. At the end of any hearing which is not attended by the young person the court should give a direction that one of the professionals involved, the guardian ad litem, solicitor or the social worker, should immediately inform the young person of the decision and provide appropriate support. These arrangements should also apply in the case of younger children. Carers, including those with whom the child or young person is placed after the proceedings, also need to be informed so that they can answer questions as they arise. Solicitors who have represented young people should always write to their clients to confirm the outcome of the proceedings and explain the effect of any decision. Without concerted efforts to explain decisions to children and young people they will continue to remain unsure about what is planned for their futures (Shaw 1998, 67).

CONCLUSION

Focusing on the child and looking at care proceedings from the standpoint of children involved in them highlights parts of the process not previously examined in studies of guardians ad litem, solicitors and court proceedings. Despite Butler-Sloss L.J.'s oft repeated statement that 'the child is a person not an object of concern', children and their concerns have been omitted from much of what has been written about court proceedings for children's protection. This study has tried to redress that balance. The number of children who could be included was small. They are not typical of children involved in these proceedings but are older and thus more able to form and express views about the processes. They cannot be said to be representative, even of the older children who are parties to public law proceedings under the Children Act. Nevertheless they are able to provide a valuable commentary; they should be heard.

These children and young people knew better than anyone what it was like for them to be the subject of care proceedings and provided with representation by a guardian ad litem and solicitor. Most could not compare their experience with previous ones, they did not know what to expect but they did want arrangements for their care to be sorted out and to be able to maintain relationships which were important to them. Their understanding may sometimes have appeared imperfect but that is as much a reflection of their representatives' and the researchers' success in communicating with them; it should not be treated as detracting from their experience.

Despite the representation system and sometimes despite considerable efforts on the part of representatives, children's concerns frequently remained unaddressed. For some children, concerns were not identified; for others, they were not vigorously advocated despite being recognised by their representatives as important for their welfare. Children were out of hearing of the legal process. One major reason for this was the court's limited power over local authority decisions, another was the desire by the professionals and particularly the court to protect children from the process itself. Overall, children and young people felt that they did not know enough about what was going on. To them the system appeared to exist for adults, not for them.

Appendix I

THE CHILDREN AND YOUNG PEOPLE IN THE STUDY

Lucy aged 10 and her younger sibling were the subject of a care order made a year previously. She had lived in two foster homes, rehabilitation had been tried unsuccessfully, and she was not able to return to her parents. A relative who lived abroad was willing to care for both children. The local authority applied to discharge the order but it was recognised that the relative needed parental responsibility. The relative was therefore encouraged to apply for a residence order. Although the children's mother originally objected to the arrangement she did not contest the final order. The children moved to live with the relative only after the order had been made.

Barbara aged 15 had been in care since early childhood. She had initially been placed transracially but had been moved from the foster carers after a number of years. She became extremely distressed and started to harm herself. The local authority obtained a secure accommodation order when Barbara was 13, and she was placed in an adolescent unit in a psychiatric hospital. She had since remained in that placement; the secure accommodation orders had been renewed regularly so that she could stay in the placement. Contact had also been re-established with her former foster carers. Barbara did not want to move from the placement and did not contest the applications to renew the orders.

Carl aged 12 had been made the subject of a care order in the previous year and placed with a relative. The local authority had not wanted a care order, a supervision order had been made in respect of a sibling who remained at home. Carl had a poor relationship with his parents, one of whom was an alcoholic. Social services arranged for Carl to return and applied for a discharge of the care order. While the proceedings were pending Carl returned to his relative who then sought legal advice and applied for a residence order.

Tom aged 12 had been made the subject of a care order when he was 5. He had lived with the same foster family since entering care, with little social services involvement. He had not seen his mother for 7 years. She applied for a contact order but Tom stated that he had no wish to see her. He and his foster carers resented social services' intrusion into their lives; the foster carers saw no role for social services other than to provide for Tom's maintenance. In the face of Tom's opposition the guardian recommended that contact should not be granted. The mother withdrew her application on the day of the hearing. Tom remained angry at the waste of time and was concerned about a future reoccurrence.

Sylvia aged 14 was the subject of care proceedings following the sudden death of her single mother. No family members were able to care for her but her grandparents tried to persuade social services to place her with foster carers whom they knew and lived close to them. Sylvia's father had recently been released after serving a prison sentence for sexual offences against her and had indicated to social services that he wanted to see her. Sylvia repeatedly indicated that she wanted contact with her father, which all the professionals opposed. The solicitor took instructions from the guardian on the basis that Sylvia was incompetent; her wish for contact was not pursued. The father did not pursue an application for contact and took no part in the care proceedings.

Edward aged 9 was the subject of care proceedings following neglect and abuse at home. He was placed with foster carers and then in a residential school because of his learning difficulties. While proceedings were pending his behaviour deteriorated, necessitating a further change in the placement arrangements. Social services planned that he should live with a relative who was already caring informally for his younger sister. This involved a move to another area and finding a suitable school for Edward. Edward had had little contact with this relative; during the proceedings he had only one further visit. When the care order was made he was still in the residential school and there was no firm date for him to move.

Peter aged 10 was the subject of care proceedings following rejection by the parent who cared for him. He had regular contact with grandparents. His original foster placement had broken down but he was happy where he was living, he wanted to remain there and stay at his current school. The care plan was not for him to stay with his present foster carers but to move to other foster carers – yet to be identified. This would probably involve a change of school. The care application was not contested. When the order was made Peter did not know what further changes this would produce for him.

Richard aged 10 was the subject of care proceedings; he had also been charged with a serious criminal offence. He was represented by the same solicitor in the care and the criminal proceedings.

Carol aged 14 with learning difficulties was the subject of care proceedings because of neglect and possible sexual abuse. She was in foster care with regular contact with her parents. She wanted to attend the court proceedings and did attend a directions hearing where the magistrates decided that she could not attend the final hearing. It would have been necessary to re-schedule this because it clashed with her holiday but the magistrates told her it would be better for her to be on holiday.

James aged 15 was the subject of a criminal supervision order, he was not the subject of a care order. The current proceedings were for the renewal of a secure accommodation order. He had been involved in some serious incidents including taking cars without consent. His relationship with his mother was poor, having deteriorated following the breakdown of her marriage, James had no contact with his stepfather whom he missed. The original secure accommodation order had been made for only 28 days because James's solicitor had been unable to take instructions. The purpose of the secure accommodation order was to ensure that James would be controlled over the school holidays. The solicitor and the guardian favoured a foster placement but the mother objected and James said he would run away. James did not oppose the renewal of the order and it was made. However, three weeks later he returned home because the secure unit said that there were no grounds for him to be detained.

Sonia aged 16 was the subject of a secure accommodation order following criminal incidents. She had a baby who was the subject of care proceedings; the local authority proposed that the baby should be placed for adoption. Sonia was so upset that she absconded from the court. She later contacted her guardian ad litem who persuaded her to give herself up. At Sonia's request the guardian in the secure accommodation proceedings sought to be appointed as Sonia's guardian in the care proceedings. She then negotiated on Sonia's behalf for a change in the care plan and for contact. The care proceedings ended with a residence order being granted to Sonia's mother.

Charles aged 9 was the subject of an uncontested application to discharge a care order. He had been living at home with his mother and her partner for some time. Charles saw the guardian twice only and the solicitor for only a few minutes.

Martin aged 14 was the subject of care proceedings. He had learning difficulties. His father had committed sexual offences against other children and Martin had alleged abuse by his stepfather and also by other children in his foster home. Martin's father sought contact but withdrew his application after an unfavourable assessment. Martin was currently in residential school with weekend placement in a temporary foster home. Long term-arrangements for his care remained uncertain although a care order was made. Subsequently a care application was made in relation to Martin's sister; a different guardian ad litem was appointed in this case.

Andrew aged 15 was the subject of care proceedings and currently fostered with relatives. He had had numerous moves; relations between him and his mother and stepfather had broken down. He had become involved in truanting and criminal activity. Andrew's parents originally opposed the care order, wanting him to return, but finally did not contest the application.

William aged 15 was the subject of a secure accommodation order. He had been in secure for 27 months on a series of orders originally made in criminal proceedings. He was a schedule 1 offender. The guardian ad litem had previously persuaded the local authority to seek a care order in relation to him; also that he should be placed in a secure establishment where he could receive therapy. William did not oppose the secure accommodation order although he indicated that he would do this when the next order was sought in three months time. He had another solicitor acting for him in criminal matters. Obtaining a care order made a crucial difference to William because it made it possible for him to stay at a secure unit with therapy; the unit did not accept young people on civil secure orders unless they were also subject to care orders.

Alex aged 9 years was the subject of care proceedings following neglect and emotional abuse by his parent and step-parent. His other parent had died some years previously. A relative who had previously obtained a residence order in relation to his sister sought and obtained a residence order for him in the care proceedings. The local authority agreed to provide an allowance to her but she had no other social work support despite living under stress. She was a single parent with the care of five children under the age of 10 years.

In addition, three children, **Alan** aged 15, **Lee** aged 13 and **Amy** aged 10, were interviewed. They were siblings of children whose cases are outlined above and were involved in the same proceedings.

One young person, **Stuart** aged 9, has not been interviewed as his case has not been concluded at court. The local authority are seeking a care order, Stuart's parents contest this. A number of assessments have been ordered. The researcher observed one visit of Stuart with his guardian ad litem, Stuart's solicitor has yet to visit him. Stuart's behaviour led to him being excluded from school and coming into care. His specialist foster placement broke down and he is now in a specialist residential unit.

Appendix II

METHOD

Research with children always raises ethical concerns, particularly about informed consent and the impact of the research process on children (Alderson 1995); research relating to children involved in the care system or in conflict with their family is particularly sensitive. The fact that there are court proceedings creates further concerns; documents in these proceedings are confidential to the court and both guardians ad litem and solicitors owe duties to the court. But if researchers regard these matters as creating insuperable barriers, children's experiences will remain personal, private and hidden.

Initially, support for conducting the research with children was canvassed with judges, court clerks, barristers, solicitors, guardians ad litem and GALRO panel managers. Despite their considerable experience, these professionals each felt uncertain of the impact they and the legal process in general had on children. All were concerned to understand more about the child's perspective on legal proceedings in which they were involved. They were also concerned that the research should be carried out in ways which recognised the particular vulnerability of children involved in specified proceedings.

APPROACH

The research was designed to focus on the child's/young person's experience of and perspective being represented in specified proceedings and include the adult representative's understanding and perspectives on their child client's experiences. Information was collected using semi-structured interviews and by observing the meetings between the children and the young people and their representatives. The researchers did not have access to case papers but attended court with its permission where the child/young person also attended.

Interviews with children and young people could only take place after the conclusion of the proceedings without risk to research confidentiality. Any statements by the child to the research could have been evidence for the proceedings and research confidentiality would have been broken if the researcher had been called to give evidence about what the child had said in interview. It was therefore not possible to interview children at different stages in the process. Interviews with children had to be kept short to maintain their interest. These interviews were designed to last no longer than half an hour. But the interviewer took her lead from the young people and spent longer if they wanted this. Interviews with representatives were planned to take place after all the cases in which they were acting had been completed so that there could be no suggestion that the interviews had influenced the child's representation. Interviews were semi-structured and covered both the experiences in the study cases and more general views and experiences of representing children. Interview schedules were developed and piloted with children and young people who had recently been the subjects of proceedings and with guardians and solicitors.

There were a number of reasons for including observation as a method. Observing meetings between children and their representatives over a period would provide the opportunity for the child to get used to the researcher; this would make it easier for the researcher to establish rapport. Children would also know that the researcher already had some knowledge about their circumstances and this might make it easier for them to talk about their experiences. Representation in care proceedings is a process which can last many months. Observation could record children's changing reactions to and views about the process; these might not be readily recalled.

YOUNG PEOPLE'S PARTICIPATION

The participation of children and young people was crucial, necessitating children's informed consent for research involvement and the establishment of a relationship where children would feel able to express their views to the researchers. We took the view that young people who could understand what researchers do and the nature of the research relationship had the legal right to consent to participating in the research (*Gillick v. W. Norfolk A.H.A.* 1986). Parental consent was not therefore required but parents needed to be informed as a matter of courtesy and their objections had to be taken seriously. We took the view that children below the age of eight would be unlikely to be able to understand these issues. With the assistance of Dr Ann Lewis, a colleague in the Institute of Education and experienced researcher of children with special educational needs, we devised two explanatory statements about the research (one intended for younger children and one for older children) for use when seeking children's agreement for the research.

RESEARCH ACCESS

Access to children and young people involved in specified proceedings, perhaps more than any others, is controlled by a series of gatekeepers who have responsibilities to safeguard the child's welfare. Recruiting children to the study necessitated convincing all these people of the merits of the research, the bona fides of the researchers and the sensitivity of the methods devised. The local authority's parental responsibility for a child in care gives it no right to prevent a competent child agreeing to participate in research. However, social services departments' uneasy relationship with guardians ad litem, their physical control of children and young people through the provision of care and their involvement in the proceedings could make it impractical to involve a child in the face of local authority objections. The courts had to be satisfied that the research would not compromise their work.

Initial approaches in the research areas were made to the directorate of the local authorities which administered the guardian ad litem panels and then to the panel managers. Support for the research was obtained from the Care Centre judge in one area, the other was informed and no objection was received. In both areas practitioners were informed through the Family Court Business Committee. The researchers gave presentations on the research to guardian ad litem panel meetings and answered subsequent queries by guardians orally and in writing.

The research could not be conducted without the cooperation of guardians ad litem and solicitors. Guardians ad litem were also in the best position to seek the child's consent, to ensure that parents were informed and to introduce the researcher to the child. Guardians were protective of the children and young people but also sensitive about research into their own practice and concerned that the research might place extra burdens on them or inhibit their work. Supporting the research could only be secondary to the guardian's main task; guardians needed to establish a relationship with the child before raising issues of research participation.

These factors were all taken into account in the research design. The researcher took the responsibility for making and maintaining contact with the guardians and solicitors. Observations were planned to start after the first meeting between the guardian and the child. The researchers also accepted that the researcher would withdraw from any meeting at the request of the guardian or the young person.

Although considerable attempts were made to inform guardians about the research via panel meetings and individually, and to satisfy them of the bona fides of the researchers and the value of the research, it was clear that a number remained unwilling to cooperate. Funding may have been an issue; the researchers did not pay the guardians for their time in interview nor for liaising with the researcher about observation meetings. Self-employed guardians may have regarded this as lost working time.

THE SAMPLE

During the research period the two panels in the study appointed guardians ad litem in 38 cases relating to 47 children over the age of 8 years. A total of 21 guardians and 20 solicitors were involved in these cases. Guardians and solicitors were also appointed for many younger children. Twenty children (involved in 17 separate sets of proceedings), their guardians (12) and solicitors (12) participated. In addition, three guardians who each had three cases which fitted the research criteria where access was not agreed were interviewed. It was not possible to observe or interview in 21 cases involving a total of 27 children over the age of 8 because the necessary permissions could not be obtained or in four cases because the very limited time between the guardian's appointment and the hearing of an application for an emergency protection order or secure accommodation order made inclusion impractical. There were seven cases where guardians considered that involving the researcher would be inappropriate, the local authority and the child each refused in one case and the parents in two. There were six further cases where a combination of factors including the guardian's involvement being put 'on hold', transfer out of the area or objections from the solicitor for the child, a child psychologist or the head of a residential school meant that the case could not be included.

Children and young people

Six girls and young women and 14 boys and young men were interviewed in the study; all were aged between 9 years and 16 years. Eighteen of the children who were interviewed were white European, two were black.

Proceedings

The 20 children were involved in 17 cases, which included all the main types of specified proceedings (Table 2).

All these applications began in the family proceedings court but three cases (all from one panel) were transferred to the county court. None of the sample cases was heard in the High Court. Of the 38 cases involving over 8s in the sample areas, 15% were heard in the county court and none in the High Court. Four of the 21 cases where there was no research access were contested, one went to the Court of Appeal. More complex cases,

Table 2:   Cases in the sample – case type

	Area 1		Area 2		Total	
	No.	*Interviews*	*No.*	*Interviews*	*No.*	*Interviews*
Secure accommodation	4	2	4	2	8	4
Care application	12	6	11	3	23	9
Others, including discharge and contact	3	2	4	2	7	4
Cases	19	10	19	7	38	17
Children interviewed		10		10		20

particularly those with conflicting expert evidence or where hearings are expected to last for more than two days, are transferred. Nationally approximately 15% of care proceedings are heard in the higher courts. None of the cases in the interview sample had a contested trial hearing; there are no published statistics on the proportion of cases at which the final hearing is uncontested. These data suggest that more complex cases were probably under-represented in the study.

Panels and solicitors

The two panels which served two shire counties and a metropolitan district included 36 guardians. Both panels included employed and fee-attracting guardians; some of the latter were also members of other panels. The nature of the areas and the fact that many of the guardians had been panel members for a number of years meant that guardians repeatedly dealt with the same social services offices. Similarly, most of the solicitors were drawn from the same geographical area and worked repeatedly with guardians on the study panels. They also did other types of legal work, generally family matters or crime, but only one regularly acted for guardians on other panels. The picture in these areas is therefore quite different from that in London where both guardians and children panel solicitors represent children in proceedings brought by many different local authorities.

FIELDWORK

All the fieldwork was conducted by Dr Maureen Winn Oakley, a solicitor with experience in child protection research and work with children and young people.

The panel administrator for each panel agreed to inform Dr Winn Oakley of all appointments of guardians to children aged 8 and over during the period 1 January 1996 to 1 September 1996. Messages were left on an answer phone which was regularly interrogated by remote access. The researcher then contacted the guardian to remind them about the study, find out about the case and make arrangements for visits if agreement was obtained. Guardians asked children if they would be willing to participate, using the information for children which the researchers had prepared if they thought it appropriate. Where participation was not obtained the researcher recorded brief details of the application and the reasons for non-participation.

When she first met the young person, the researcher checked with them that they were still willing to participate. Before she interviewed the children and young people she checked again that each one understood the nature of her role as a researcher and agreed to be interviewed. All children and young people were assured that nothing they said would be repeated to their guardian or solicitor unless they asked for this to be done. All children and young people were made aware that research involvement would not affect their cases or situation.

Apart from the guardian's first meeting Dr Winn Oakley attended almost all meetings between the child and solicitor or guardian, visiting the place where the child was currently living and participating in outings to McDonald's etc. On three occasion meetings were missed because they clashed with others for the study. One guardian arranged to see a child alone on one occasion to discuss disclosures of child sexual abuse and one solicitor saw a child without the researcher to discuss issues relating to separate criminal proceedings. In all, the researcher attended 63 meetings lasting between 10 minutes and two hours. The majority of visits took place at the child's home after school. Children attending residential school were seen at school, sometimes at the end of the school day; young people in secure accommodation were seen there and at court when they attended their court hearing. The researcher aimed to be an inconspicuous observer at all meetings, not an easy task in cramped homes, but some children insisted that she participate in games or wanted to show her their life-story books, pictures or toys. Research notes were not taken at the meetings but written immediately afterwards, usually in the car. On occasion the researcher arrived at the venue before either the solicitor or the guardian, who had been delayed by earlier appointments or in court. If she had not visited the child before she waited outside so that the representative could introduce her.

Interviews with children were held shortly after the proceedings had been completed. Most interviews were held where the child was living; one child was interviewed at McDonald's. All but one child agreed to tape recording of the interview. Interviews with children ranged from 10 minutes to an hour, those with professionals between one and one and a half hours. Interviews with professionals all took place after they had ceased to be involved in the proceedings relating to the child in the study. With the exception of one guardian all interviews were tape-recorded.

CASE LIST

A. v. Liverpool C.C. [1982] A.C. 363 H.L.
B. (care: contact: local authority's plans), Re [1993] 1 F.L.R. 543.
B. (minors)(contact), Re [1994] 2 F.L.R. 1 C.A.
B. (minors)(local authority: representation), Re [1996] 1 F.L.R. 56.
B. v. B. (court bundles: video evidence) [1994] 1 F.L.R. 323.
B. v. Derbyshire C.C. [1992] 1 F.L.R. 538.
Berkshire C.C. v. B. [1997] 1 F.L.R. 171.
C. (a minor) (child's wishes), Re [1993] 1 F.L.R. 832.
C. (expert evidence: disclosure practice), Re [1995] 1 F.L.R. 204.
C. (interim order: residential assessment), Re [1997] 1 F.L.R. 1 H.L.
C. v. Solihull M.B.C. [1993] 1 F.L.R. 290.
Cheshire C.C. v. M. [1993] 1 F.L.R. 463.
D. (secure accommodation order), Re [1997] 1 F.L.R. 197.
Devon C.C. v. S. [1992] 2 F.L.R. 244.
G. (a minor)(care proceedings), Re [1994] 2 F.L.R. 69.
Gillick v. W. Norfolk A.H.A. [1986] A.C. 112.
H. v. Cambridgeshire C.C. [1996] 2 F.L.R. 566.
Hounslow L.B.C. v. A. [1993] 1 F.L.R. 702.
Humberside C.C. v. D.P.R. [1977] 3 All E.R. 964.
J. (minors)(care: care plan), Re [1994] 1 F.L.R. 253.
L.H. (a minor)(wardship jurisdiction), Re [1986] 2 F.L.R. 306.
London Borough of Croydon v. R. [1997] 2 F.L.R. 675.
M. (secure accommodation), Re [1996] 1 F.L.R. 418 C.A.
Manchester City Council v. B. [1996] 1 F.L.R. 324.
Newham L.B.C. v. A.G. [1993] 1 F.L.R. 281 C.A.
Oxfordshire C.C. v. M. [1994] 2 All E.R. 269.
P. (minors)(interim orders), Re [1993] 2 F.L.R. 742.
Practice Direction [1994] 1 F.L.R. 108.
Practice Note [1993] 2 F.L.R. 641.
President's Practice Note: Case Management [1995] 1 F.L.R. 456.
President's Direction [1993] 1 F.L.R. 668.
R. v. Birmingham C.C. ex p. A. [1997] 2 F.L.R. 841.
R. v. Cornwall C.C. ex p. G. [1992] 1 F.L.R. 270.
R. v. Kingston upon Thames R.B.C. ex p. T. [1994] 1 F.L.R. 798.
R. v. Worthing Justices ex p. Stevenson [1976] 2 All E.R. 194.

S.(independent representation), Re [1993] 2 F.L.R. 437.

Stockport M.B.C. v. D. [1995] 1 F.L.R. 873.

T. (a minor)(guardian ad litem: case record), Re [1994] 1 F.L.R 632 F.D. and C.A.

T. (a minor)(care order: conditions), Re [1994] 2 F.L.R. 423.

T. (a minor)(termination of contact: discharge of order), Re [1997] 1 All E.R. 169 C.A.

W. (secure accommodation order: attendance at court), Re [1994] 2 F.L.R. 1092.

BIBLIOGRAPHY

ABA (1995) American Bar Association proposed standards of practice for lawyers who represent children in abuse and neglect cases. *Family Law Quarterly* **29**: 375–405.

ABAFA (1979) *Care Proceedings*. Report of the Legal Group Working Party, ABAFA, London.

Alderson, P. (1995) *Listening to Children. Children, Ethics and Social Research*. Barnardos, Essex.

Alston, P., Parker, S. and Seymour, J. (eds) (1992) *Children, Rights and the Law*. Clarendon, Oxford.

Anderson, R. (1978) *Representation in the Juvenile Court*. RKP, London.

Association of Lawyers for Children (ALC) (1996) Child Care Conference. *Family Law* **26**: 767–768.

Association of Lawyers for Children (ALC) (1998) The future of representation for children. *Family Law* **28**; 403–411.

BAAF (1997) *Interference or Rubber Stamp? The function of the court in child care cases.* Legal Group AGM Seminar 1995, BAAF.

Bainham, A. (1990) The privatisation of the public interest in children. *Modern Law Review* **53**: 206–221.

Bainham, A. (1993) *Children: The Modern Law*. Sweet and Maxwell, London.

Barn, R. (1993) *Black Child in the Public Care System*. Batsford, London.

Bean, P. and Melville, J. (1989) *Lost Children of the Empire*. Unwin Hyman, London.

Blumberg, A. (1967) The practice of law as a confidence game. *Law and Society Review* **1**(2): 15–39.

Booth, M. (1996) *Avoiding Delay in Children Act Cases*. Lord Chancellor's Department, London.

Booth, T. and Booth, W. (1996) Supported parenting for people with learning difficulties. Lessons from Wisconsin. *Representing Children* **9**(2): 99–107.

Brasse, G. (1996) The confidentiality of a child's instructions. *Family Law* **26**: 733–735.

Bridges, L., Meszaros, G. and Sunkin, M. (1995) *Judicial Review in Perspective*. Cavendish, London.

Butler, I. and Williamson, H. (1994) *Children Speak*. Longman, Harlow, Essex.

CAAC (1992) *Children Act Advisory Committee Annual Report 1991–2*. Lord Chancellor's Department, London.

CAAC (1994) *Children Act Advisory Committee Annual Report 1993–4*. Lord Chancellor's Department, London.

CAAC (1995) *Children Act Advisory Committee Annual Report 1994–5*. Lord Chancellor's Department, London.

CAAC (1997) *The Children Act Advisory Committee Final Report*. Lord Chancellor's Department, London.

CAAC (1997a) *Handbook of Best Practice in Children Act Cases*. Lord Chancellor's Department, London.

Cain, M. (1979) The general practice lawyer and the client; towards a radical conception *International Journal of the Sociology of Law* **7**: 331–354.

Cashmore, J. and Bussey, K. (1994) Perceptions of children and lawyers in care and protection proceedings. *International Journal of Law and the Family* **8**: 319–336.

Clark, D.J. (1995) *Whose Case Is It Anyway?* Master of Philosophy Thesis, University of Sussex.

Clark, D.J. (1995a) Child Panel under fire. *Law Society Gazette 92/37:* 1.

Collier, J. (1997) Children's rights. *New Law Journal,* July 18: 1060, 1072.

Cretney S. and Masson J. (1997) *Principles of Family Law* (6th edn). Sweet and Maxwell, London.

Dewar, J. (1995) The courts and local authority autonomy. *Child and Family Law Quarterly* **7**(2): 15–25.

DH (1990) *An Introduction to the Children Act 1989.* HMSO, London.

DH (1991) *The Children Act 1989. Guidance and Regulations. Vol 1 Court Orders.* HMSO, London.

DH (1991a) *Working Together under the Children Act 1989.* HMSO, London.

DH (1991b) *The Children Act and the Courts – a guide for children and young people* (Leaflet CAG6). Department of Health, London.

DH (1992) *Children Act Report 1992* (Cm 2144). HMSO, London.

DH (1992a) *Manual of Practice Guidance for Guardians Ad Litem and Reporting Officers.* HMSO, London.

DH (1992b) *The Guardian Ad Litem and Reporting Officer Service Annual Reports 1991–1992. An Overview.* Department of Health, London.

DH (1995) *Guide for Guardians Ad Litem in Public Law Proceedings under the Children Act 1989.* HMSO, London.

DH (1995a) *Not Alone: a children's guide to care proceedings.* HMSO, London.

DH (1995b) *Child Protection Messages From Research.* HMSO, London.

DH (1995c) *The Guardian Ad Litem And Reporting Officer Service. Annual Reports 1994–1995. An Overview.* Department of Health, London.

DH (1996) *Implementing National Standards – a guide through quality assurance for the guardian service.* Department of Health, London

DH and WO (1995) *National Standards for Guardians ad Litem.* Department of Health, London.

DH and WO (1996) *The Guardian ad Litem and Reporting Officer Service Complaints. Working Party Report.* SSI, Department of Health and Welsh Office, London.

DH, HO, LCD and WO (1998) Support services in family proceedings – future organisations of court welfare services. Department of Health, London.

DHSS (1974) *Report of the Committee of Inquiry into the Care and Supervision Provided in Relation to Maria Colwell.* HMSO, London.

DHSS (1985) *Review of Child Care Law.* HMSO, London.

Dingwall, R. and Eekelaar, J. (1983) *The Protection of Children.* Blackwell, Oxford.

Eekelaar, J. (1986) The emergence of children's rights. *Oxford Journal of Legal Studies* **6**: 161–182.

Eekelaar, J. (1992) The importance of thinking that children have rights. *International Journal of Law and the Family* **6**(1): 221–235. (reprinted in Alston et al, above).

European Convention (1995) European Convention on the Exercise of Children's Rights and Explanatory Report. *Representing Children* **8**(4): 9–29.

Farnfield, S. and Kaszap, M. (1998) What makes a helpful grown up? Children's views of professionals in mental health services. *Health Informatics* 4.2: 1–12.

Farson, R. (1978) *Birthrights.* Penguin Books, Harmondsworth.

Faulkner, A. (1995) Are children's voices really heard in family proceedings? *British Juvenile and Family Courts Society Newsletter* 13–12-95.

Felstiner, W., Abel, R. and Sarat, A. (1981) The emergence and transformation of disputes: naming, blaming and claiming. *Law and Society Review* **15**: 631–654.

Fortin, J. (1998) *Children's Rights and the Developing Law*. Butterworths, London.

Freeman, M.D.A. (1983) *The Rights and Wrongs of Children*. Frances Pinter, London.

Freeman, P. (1994) *Parents' Perceptions of Care Proceedings*. Socio-legal Centre for Family Studies, University of Bristol, mimeograph.

Galanter, M. (1974) Why the 'haves' come out ahead: speculations on the limits of legal change. *Law and Society Review* **9**: 95–160.

Genn, H. and Genn, Y. (1989) *The Effectiveness of Representation at Tribunals*. Lord Chancellor's Department, London.

Goldstein, J., Freud, A. and Solnit, A. (1973) *Beyond the Best Interests of the Child*. Free Press, New York.

Hamilton, I. (1997) Guardians ad litem and the separate representation of children. Political change a cause for concern? *Representing Children* **10**(2): 72–75.

Hayes, M. (1996) The proper role of the courts in child care cases. *Child and Family Law Quarterly* **8**: 201–216.

Hilgendorf, L. (1981) *Social Workers and Solicitors in Child Care Cases*. HMSO, London.

Holt, J. (1975) *Escape from Childhood*. Penguin Books, Harmondsworth.

Hoon, G. (1997) Address to National Association of Guardians ad Litem and Reporting Officers Conference, Bath.

Hoon, G. (1998) Address to Solicitors Family Law Association Annual Conference, Blackpool.

Hunt, J. (1993) *Local Authority Wardships Before the Children Act: the Baby or the Bathwater?* HMSO, London.

Hunt, J. and Macleod A. (1997) *The Last Resort*. Centre for Socio-legal Studies, University of Bristol.

Irvine, D. (1997) Role of the family. *New Law Journal* March 21: 408.

Jackson, D. (1997) Letter to Lord Irvine. *Representing Children* **10**(1): 6–9.

Judicial Statistics (1996) *Judicial Statistics Annual Report 1996* (1997 Cm 3716). HMSO, London.

King, M. (1971) *Bail or Custody*. The Cobden Trust, London.

King, P. and Young, I. (1992) *The Child as Client. A Handbook for Solicitors who Represent Children*. Family Law, Bristol.

Lansdown, G. (1995) *Taking Part. Children's Participation in Decision Making*. Consent Series 1. Institute For Public Policy Research, London.

Law Society (1979) *Memorandum on Representation of Children in Care Proceedings*. Law Society, London.

Law Society (1994) *Attendance of Solicitors at Child Protection Conferences*. Guidance Issued by The Law Society's Family Law Committee, London.

Law Society (1994a) *Guidance on Acting for Children in Private Law Proceedings under the Children Act 1989*. Law Society, London.

Legal Aid Board (1997) Matrimonial family guidance revision. *Legal Aid Focus* **19**: 4–18.

Liddle, C. (1992) *Acting for Children. The Law Society's Handbook for Solicitors and Guardians Ad Litem Working with Children*. The Law Society, London.

Lindley, B. (1994) *Families in Court*. Family Rights Group, London.

Lyon, C. and Parton, N. (1995) Children's rights and the Children Act 1989. In Franklin, B. (ed) *The Handbook of Children's Rights*. Routledge, London.

MacCormick, N. (1976) Children's rights: a test case for theories of rights. *Archiv Für Rechts und Socialphilosophie* **62**: 305–316.

Macleod, A. (1989) *Representation of the Child in Civil Proceedings – the Legal Perspective*. Socio-legal Centre for Family Studes, University of Bristol.

Macleod, A. and Malos, E. (1984) *Representation of Children and Parents in Care Proceedings*. Family Law Research Unit, University of Bristol.

McConville, M., Bridges, L. and Pavlovic, A. (1994) *Standing Accused*. Clarendon Press, Oxford.

Maidment, S. (1981) The fragmentation of parental rights of children in care. *Journal of Social Welfare Law* **3**: 21–35.

Masson, J. (1992) The Official Solicitor as the child's guardian ad litem. *Journal of Child Law* **4**: 58–62.

Masson, J. (1996) Representations of children. *Current Legal Problems* **49**: 245–265.

Masson, J. and Harrison, C. (1996) Identity: mapping the frontiers. In Lowe, N. and Douglas, G. (eds) *Families across Frontiers*. Martinus Nijhoff, The Hague.

Masson, J. and Morris, M. (1992) *Children Act Manual*. Sweet and Maxwell, London.

Masson, J. and Morton S. (1989) The use of wardship by local authorities. *Modern Law Review* **52**: 762–789.

Masson, J. and Shaw, M. (1988) The work of guardians ad litem. *Journal of Social Welfare Law* **10:** 164–184.

Masson, J., Norbury, D. and Chatterton, S. (1984) *Mine, Yours or Ours?* HMSO, London.

Masson, J., Harrison, C. and Pavlovic, A. (1997) *Working Towards Partnership with Lost Parents*. J. Rowntree Foundation, York.

Moore, C. and Lane, M. (1992) *Meeting Your Guardian ad Litem*. The Children's Society, London.

Moore, J. (1985) *The ABC of Child Abuse Work*. Gower, Aldershot.

Murch, M. (1987) *The Length of Care Proceedings*. Socio-legal Centre for Family Studies, University of Bristol.

Murch, M. and Hooper, D. (1992) *The Family Justice System* Family Law, Bristol.

Murch M., Hunt, J. and Macleod, A. (1989) *Representation of the Child in Civil Courts. Research Project Care Proceedings: the Legal Perspective, Draft Report*. Socio-legal Centre for Family Studies, University of Bristol.

Murch, M., Hunt, J. and Macleod, A. (1990) *The Representation of the Child in Civil Proceedings Research Project 1985–89: Summary of Conclusions and Recommendations*. Socio-legal Centre for Family Studies, University of Bristol.

NSPCC (1993) *The Child Witness Pack*. NSPCC, London.

O'Donovan, K. (1993) *Family Law Matters*. Pluto Press, London.

O'Neill, O. (1992) Children's rights and children's lives. *International Journal of Law and the Family* **61**: 24–42 (reprinted in Alston et al, above).

Parker, H., Casburn, M. and Turnbull, D. (1981) *Receiving Juvenile Justice*. Basil Blackwell, Oxford.

Riches, P. (1997) Reporting to the court under the Children Act 1989. *Children Services News* **8**: Supplement.

Sarat, A. and Felstiner, W. (1986) Law and strategy in the divorce lawyer's office. *Law and Society Review* **20**(1): 93–134.

Sawyer, C. (1995) *The Rise and Fall of the Third Party*. Centre for Socio-Legal Studies, Oxford.

SFLA (1984) Solicitors Family Law Association Code of Practice. *Family Law* **14**: 156–7.

SFLA (1995) *Guide to Good Practice For Solicitors Acting for Children* (2nd edn). SFLA.

Shaw, C. (1998) *Remember My Messages . . . Who Cares?* Trust, London. Somerset Area Review Committee (1979) *Wayne Brewer – Report of the Review Panel*. Somerset Area Review Committee, Taunton.

Thorpe, M. and Clarke, E. (eds) (1998) *Divided Duties*. Family Law, Bristol.

Timms, J. (1995) *Children's Representation*. Sweet and Maxwell, London.

Waller, B. (1997) Working in the family courts – a social work perspective. *Family Law* **27**: 191–193.

Wells, T. (1995) The child's best interests v procedures. *Family Law* **25**: 193–194.

White, R., Carr, P. and Lowe, N. (1995) *A Guide to the Children Act 1989* (2nd edn). Butterworths, London.

Winn Oakley, M. (1998) Approaching the Millennium – Representing Young People. In Poyser, A. (ed) *Approaching the Millennium – Children and the Guardian Service Within the Family Justice System*. Panel Managers Annual Workshop. Department of Health, London.

Winn Oakley, M. (1998a) What do young people think of those who represent them in care proceedings. *Practioners Child Law Bulletin*, **11**(5): 56–59.

INDEX